THOSE CRAZY

GIANTS FANS!

First Printing: July 1983

Inquiries should be addressed to:
Irv Brechner Targeted Marketing Inc.
P.O. Box 453
Livingston NJ 07039

ISBN O-9611578-0-1

Commercial Photo Credits

Tom Christie:	1, 2, 3, 4, 9A, 10A, 10B, 11, 12, 28, 32, 36, 37, 38, 39
Linda Bohm:	164, 165, 166, 167, 168, 169, 170, 173
Joe McKenna:	34
The Record:	4, 8, 9B, 15, 64 (2), 66
1963 Giants Yearbook:	29

Some very special thankyous...

This book was a real labor of love, not only on my part, but by the number of people that cooperated to see it become a reality. I can't thank enough the Giants management and players for their wonderful assistance, plus everyone else and the fans listed below.

GIANTS STAFF
Tom Power
Ed Croke
Jim Gleason
Ed Wagner
Ed Wagner Jr.
Pat Wagner

NFL PROPERTIES
Jim Noel & Staff

NJ SPORTS AUTHORITY
Bob Castronovo
Stan Gorlak
Bill Kohm
Les Unger
George Wirt

PHOTOGRAPHERS
Linda Bohm
Tom Christie
Joe McKenna

SPORTS WRITERS
Dave Anderson
Vinny DiTrani
Dave Klein
Jim Smith

GIANTS PLAYERS/COACHES
Billy Ard
Jeff Baldiner
Brad Benson
Tom Bresnahan
Scott Brunner
Brian Carpenter
Rob Carpenter
Harry Carson
Joe Danelo
Floyd Eddings
Ron Erhardt
Larry Flowers
Larry Heater
Ernie Hughes
Bruce Kimball
Gordon King
Sylvester McGrew
Tom Mullady
Bill Parcells
Johnny Perkins
Danny Pittman
Beasley Reece
Roy Simmons
Brad Van Pelt
Mike Whittington

SPECIAL CONTRIBUTORS
Rose Albanese
Howard Brechner
Dave Burke
Henry DiBianchi
Dr. Elaine Eden
Neil Ginsberg
Dr. Michael Givant
Ed Goldstein
Mitch Goodhue
Bill Jacobowitz
Fiori Paluscio
Corky Raab
Tom Scott
Jack Sheperd
Ed Sulem

THE FANS
Ed Ball
Al Barrett
Mitch Bator
Mr. & Mrs. Alex Berger
Allan Berman
Walter Blum
Joan Bowen
Leo Bruck
Richard Carbone Jr.
John Cook
James DiGesu
Robert Drossman
Michael Evers
Bart Fellin
Charlie Farrenkopf
Lee Fernandes
Doreen & Norman
 Fishkin
Lou & Sue Foster
Bill Freda
John Gibbons
Jack Goellner
Ron and Cathy Haldas
Don & Marilyn Heiner
David Humphreys Sr.
 & Family
Jim Kartails

James Kearns
Stuart Landau
Michael Lesco
Robert Lopa
Eric Lund
Patti Magee
Robert Mahar
Nancy Mangieri
Gary Marzolla
Richard McDonnell
Gene McNevins
Richard Mulvey
Bob Murphy
Charles Nash Jr.
Dee Nixon
Frank Roberts
Bert Rosenkrantz
Paul Ruller
Joy Shue
Charles Stelzer
Chris Sullivan
Daniel Timoney
Ralph Vaiatica
Martin Wall
Bev Wills
Stuart Wolff
Ken Zelenakas

Dedication

To the world's largest fraternity, a group as diverse as can be, may we all share the biggest fantasy imaginable: a 1984 Super Bowl victory!

and

To my wife Kathi, who, with other Giants fans' spouses, understands the fanatacism that is uniquely ours.

THOSE CRAZY

GIANTS FANS!

Contents

CHAPTER 1

How this whole thing got started

How This Whole Thing Got Started

My sole reason for writing this book is to get a pair of season tickets for the Giants.

Well, almost. Actually, you'd be surprised at what lengths people go to in their attempt to get Giant tickets to a game, let alone season tickets. And when they get season tickets, they never let them go . . . so many of them are willed from generation to generation.

These are fans that go beyond the call of duty. These are people that are normal, healthy and decent citizens: bankers, lawyers, teachers, factory workers, bartenders and salesmen. But come Sunday afternoon they become crazed with Giant fever. They become addicts; they assume personalities and roles you wouldn't believe. They forget about money worries, marriage problems and anything "normal" people have to contend with. For three hours every Sunday afternoon, nothing, not even an atomic blast, interrupts their devotion.

One night, after a particularly wonderful Giants victory, I caught the highlights on no less than 7 TV stations, and Betamaxed them to form a 10 minute tape of sheer ecstasy. I watched the same touchdown pass 4 times in a row, and loved every second of it! I also started wondering if I was the only crazy Giant fan.

When I started asking around, I found my devotion (considered by some to be quite strong) paled by comparison to what some people do to follow this team.

When I started asking true blue Giant fans about a book of their escapades, they loved it! "What can I do to help?", "How can I assist you?" and "Call so and so" were the only answers I got. The letters started pouring in, every day, bringing stories you wouldn't believe. Things I, as a die-hard, almost couldn't believe. But they were usually accompanied by pictures, so I knew they weren't fabricated.

And all the letters started off the same way: "My husband is the greatest Giants fan"; "I am the #1 fan"; "My dad is the most die-hard, loyal Giants fan there is." Everyone claimed to be #1, the best, the ultimate. It was tough, but I chose our very own ultimate Giants fan, Mr. Ed Sulem of Gloversville, New York (see chapter 7).

I heard from people where hearing or seeing a game was a real hardship—from as far north as New Hampshire, as far south as Florida, as far west as California and as far east as . . . England! Yes, and do you have any idea what time Monday night football is on in Britain?

I was sent pictures of tailgate parties that some people would pay to get into . . . and pictures of groups of people in home and away Giant jerseys. And heartwarming pictures

2

of people who not only did crazy things, but wonderful things (see chapter 8).

Most of all, I received a sense of what sport is all about from the people in the stands. I learned what devotion really is; how people share a bond that cuts across every ethnic, racial or religious line. I felt the texture of family that somehow is so ingrained despite the win/loss record of the Giants in recent memory.

But one nagging question remained and bothered me: Why?

Why are we the way we are?

Why are we late to our own engagement parties, weddings and other special events because some group of men took too much time knocking each other senseless on a football field?

Why do we refuse to ever give up rooting for this team? Why did we not move to Dallas or Philadelphia after "The Fumble" like most sane people would have? Why do we put tickets in our wills and make the scalpers rich? Why, why, why?

For thoughts on this perplexing question, I turned to the Giants players, coaches and management, our fine area sportswriters, a local psychologist and a sociologist from Adelphi University. Their insights and pet theories (found in Chapter 9) make for very interesting reading.

I tell ya . . . this book was a real trip. The mail I received, the stories I heard, the people who went out of their way to help are just not to be believed.

This project was fun, no hysterical. And heartwarming, unbelievable and amazing. I felt like an archeologist uncovering a new counterculture. But most of all it was a tribute . . . to the world's largest fraternity of men and women of all ages, perhaps linked together by fate or a bacteria which strikes certain people and lasts for life. This book is a real curtain call for . . .

THOSE CRAZY GIANTS FANS!!!

P.S. Tickets anyone?

CHAPTER 2

No matter
the weather
it's tailgate time!

Tailgating Giants Style

The word itself means comraderie, excitement and light-and-lively fun. And that's just what tailgating at Giants football games has come to mean. From the two buddies drinking beer and eating chicken out of the trunk of the car, to the elaborate float-like parties featuring sit-down meals, tailgaters at Giants games are another breed, sort of a sub-division of general Giants fans!

According to Les Unger, Director of Public Relations for the stadium and arena, "tailgating, which has been going on for many years in many places, was originally encouraged by us as a partial solution to the traffic problem. We wanted people to stay 5–6 hours, make a day of it, and not rush out after the game or come zooming in at 5 minutes to one o'clock."

Well, tailgating has taken off, to the tune of over 15,000 people participating every Sunday. A full one third of all the fans show up before noon to begin the festivities, and it, for many, has become a big social event.

Among the thousands of cars parked, you'll find campers, busses, tents, umbrellas and canopies, all brightly decorated, popping up like flowers in the spring.

There have been some remarkable tailgate parties through the years, and several years ago, a contest was held, with trophies awarded by local sportswriters and food editors, who sampled the fare.

Some of the more outstanding entries included a Rolls Royce tailgate party, a tailgate party with a beautiful painting, a party with china and crystal and a former restauranteur who prepared 24 different varieties of foods with uniformed bartenders serving!

The food at these parties is not limited to burgers, dogs and beer. We've seen it all, including clams on the half shell, lobsters, steaks, shish kabob and more! Dessert is no exception, with elaborate cakes, sometimes in the shape of the field, and one memorable one complete with little figurines.

Inclement weather does not deter these loyal, fun loving fans. Tailgating goes on during rain or snow. There's only one real problem—many tailgaters take up several parking spots, parking across the lines instead of between them. As more and more people get into tailgating, someday the stadium will run out of spots, so let's try and keep that down to a minimum, folks!

Tailgating has become a way of life for many . . . a real fun thing to do on a crisp fall day, with a light wind blowing under clear blue skies. If you haven't tried it, try it . . . you'll love it!

It's tailgate row, as the cars, tables, coolers all line up before Giants games.

Tailgating on Route 17

Corky Raab (see Chapter 8) was coming home after one Giant game, when he was stopped by an accident on Route 17 north. Traffic was completely halted on all the lanes, and everything was at a standstill until the accident was cleared.

It was late, and everyone on the road had just come out of the stadium. One guy spotted Corky's Budwewiser van, and shouted "Do you have any beer left?"

Well, Corky did, and said "Yes . . . all you Giants fans come on over." He recalls, "There we were on Route 17, drinking beer and talking football." It was a tailgate party in the unlikeliest of places.

With the stadium in the background, tailgaters enjoy the festivities.

The Goshen (NY) group sits down for a nice pregame lunch, complete with tablecloth, candleabra and delicious food.

Blasting off on another Sunday. The sign says "One small step for the Giants . . . One Giant step to Super Bowl."

Giants fans unveil the secret weapon: the Giant beetle! Must be refilled with gas during halftime.

A Brad Van Pelt lookalike pierces the Redskins teepee in this creative endeavor.

Walter Blum and his group enjoy burgers and dogs . . . tailgate style.

More of the crowd enjoying tailgating.

CHAPTER 3

Tickets anyone?

Season tickets . . . people will do anything for them . . . and I mean anything!

The Real Ticket Story . . .

The Giants have the most loyal fans, without question. And this manifests itself in a problem any other team would love to have: a waiting list for season tickets. But the Giants' management is very sensitive to this issue, and here are some interesting facts you might find enlightening:

. . .One of the primary reasons why the Giants left Yankee Stadium was what would have happened to their ticket holders if they stayed. According to PR Director Tom Power, "If we had stayed there, two things would have happened after they refurbished the stadium. There would have been about 6,000 less seats for football, and the shape of the field would have been changed. Not only would we have had to send 'sold out' notices to many of our fans, but people sitting on the 50 yard line might have ended up sitting in the end zone. It wouldn't have been a good situation for our fans."

. . ."People don't understand why there are very few new season ticket holders. Fewer than 100 tickets turn over in any given year. The fans are just unbelievably loyal."

. . .The ticket prices for Giants seats are among the lowest in the NFL.

. . ."We don't have any requirement as to where tickets can be mailed to," according to Power. "We mail tickets to all the New England states; we have a number of European addresses. These people don't give their tickets up . . . they know they're coming back."

. . .About 85 percent of the season ticket holders are from New York or New Jersey. That leaves about 10,000 people that come from out of the area! Says Tom, "A lot of people come from Connecticut, Massachusetts, Pennsylvania, South Jersey, the Poconos."

. . .There are over 10,000 people on the waiting list (not counting those who've given up), and over 1,000 on the list for suites . . . those glass enclosed boxes that go for a pretty penny.

. . .People place ads in football papers looking to buy tickets for one or two years from people that have been tempo-
rarily transferred.

. . .Giants fans support the team, even on away trips. "In
most every Stadium we play", according to Young, "Giants
fans materialize in the stands. They come out to support us
no matter where we are."

The Giants' management really doesn't have any alterna-
tives when it comes to season tickets. They really can't add
more seats to the current ballpark, but what they are doing,
after so many disappointing years, is to draft quality players, bring in top coaching talent, and make this team what
the fans want: a winner!

Ticket Shorts . . .

Without question, the ultimate goal for everyone other
than the lucky 73,000 season ticket holders is to somehow
get Giants tickets (see first line of my introduction to this
book).

In the course of my research, I've come across a bunch of
interesting stories about the crazy things us fans do to get
into the stadium.

. . ."People will do anything to see the Dallas game. We
saw one guy buy four tickets from a scalper, at $250 . . . yes
two-hundred-fifty-dollars . . . per ticket!"

. . ."People have tickets in their wills. And we know some
people that had them in their divorce settlement. Forget
custody of the kids, the issue is who gets the tickets."

. . ."The president of a corporation was retiring, on a very
large pension, with a condo In Florida, a Caddy . . . everything the guy could want. But his largest concern was that
the corporation's season tickets be a part of the retirement
package."

. . ."We have payed scalpers nearly $1200 over the last 5
years (on the average of $30 a game for 8 home games per
year). We know all the scalpers by name."

. . ."We would only apply for jobs at companies that we
knew had a season box. Anything for a ticket!"

. . ."We went as far as buying season tickets for the new New Jersey Generals team this year. Our hopes are that Herschel Walker will steal enough borderline Giants fans (are there any?) away so that some season tickets will open up for us. Anybody wanna trade?"

. . ."One guy stole 600 tickets from the mail several years back. The postal inspectors are always at every game. This poor guy got caught . . . he was out personally scalping the tickets . . . and he had the mailbag right in his car!"

Swiss Account

For 15 years Leo Bruck has been working in a little town called Zug, for a company called Phlipp Brothers. If you guessed that Zug is in Switzerland, you're right, and owning a pair of Giants tickets, Leo had a dilemna.

The regulations state that if you transfer Giants tickets to another name, you lose them. So, knowing he would return someday, Leo couldn't transfer the tickets to anyone.

In order to get around this problem, the Giants airmail his tickets to his Swiss address every year. Upon receipt, Leo mails them back to people in the states who use them in his absence.

According to Leo, "This effort has now paid off since I just moved back to the states at the beginning of the year, and now will be able to enjoy seeing the Giants in person."

But that's not all of Leo's story. Even though he couldn't see the games in person, he still saw them on TV. He had an American color TV and video tape recorder sent to him in Switzerland, since the European and American models are not compatible. Friends in the U.S. would tape the games and send him the casettes! What a way to go!

Now that Leo's back in the country, he hopes that "they will rise out of the ashes of the last several years and go on to great heights to become a power in the NFL!" Couldn't agree more!

Don't Play Games With Giants Fans!

Michael Evers and his dad are on the never ending waiting list for season tickets. So when GAMES magazine ran a contest asking for funny football captions, with two NFL season tickets as the prize, the Evers entered. What the heck, they figured, it was worth a little thought and 20 cents postage.

Well, they won, and die-hards father and son told GAMES Magazine they wanted Giants tickets. Which, of course, the magazine couldn't get. That's where the fun started.

GAMES insisted that the Evers take other tickets or the monetary equivalent. According to Mike, "There is no monetary equivalent to Giants tickets."

The magazine finally contacted Tim Mara, and after a years' wait, Mike and Richard got their tickets! Lock city, you say, right? The story doesn't end there.

Michael continues the tale. "The magazine told us the tickets were not renewable. This, I could not bear to hear! We had no intention of ever watching another home game on TV. So my dad wrote to Tim Mara asking for renewal rights, which, to my amazement, were granted."

The moral of the story is: never underestimate the power of Giants fans!

The Ticket That Never Would Be . . .

Nancy Mangieri of New Windsor, New York relates a story that is both touching and heartbreaking. Nancy's wedding gift to her husband-to-be was a pair of Giant season tickets.

A true romantic he grabbed her tenderly and said "If I had known you were giving me these tickets, I'd have married you much sooner!" That's where the story begins.

It seems that the Mangieri's sat next to the same couple in Yankee Stadium, the Yale Bowl, and finally when they settled down in Giants Stadium. Their neighbors were getting on in years by the time the team moved to the Meadowlands, and the Mangieri's had four children since they first became neighbors in the house that Ruth built.

Anyhow, the other couple, who had no children, obtained a third ticket, which they gave to their father, who passed away shortly thereafter. So there was an empty seat, which, after expressing sympathy, looked very inviting to the Mangieri's. Nancy gingerly asked to purchase the open seat.

The Mangieri's learned the true meaning of sentimentality when the other couple buried their father . . . along with the ticket! Now isn't that something!

Anything For Tickets

Two brothers had been attending Giants games since 1939, when they were in their teens. Throughout the years, they moved from the Polo Grounds to Yankee Stadium.

At one point, they sat next to people who owned six tickets. This family shared the same heritage—being Giants fans from the start. These people were planning to retire in 1972, and the husband wanted the brothers to have the tickets since the couple knew the brothers had a total of eight children.

During the winter after the 1970 season, the husband died of a heart attack. The promise of the six tickets followed him to the grave.

One of the brothers picks up the story. "Being a resourceful salesman, I reminded her of the promise in a tactful way; my brother and I made a lunch date with her at Lutece in New York. After a lunch costing about $135.00, I appealed to her sense of fair play. Finally, after having dropped my brother off at his law office, I dropped the lady off in front of St. Patrick's cathedral, where I had extracted a promise for getting two of the six tickets. Every time we go to a Giant game, despite the fact we now have four tickets on the 35 yard line, I still look at the four next to us . . . knowing they should have been ours."

These two brothers and their families get together a lot during football season; their father was the catering manager for Harry M. Stevens at both the Polo Grounds and Yankee Stadium. Well maybe there is a way to get the rest of the clan into the stadium . . . "beer here!"

CHAPTER 4

The fans
in the stands
are grand.

The Scranton Connection

Every summer, David Humphreys and his family pack their bags and head for a much deserved two week vacation. As they head east from Scranton, Pennsylvania, they have before them many different interesting places to spend their time off.

Karen today, and as a five year old in the arms of Tarkenton.

Among the choices are the fresh, cool Poconos, the Jersey shore with the glimmering lights of Atlantic City, the excitement of the Big Apple or the beauty of Cape Cod.

David Humphreys, his wife, daughter and son have no intention of visiting these typical tourist spots. No . . . they are headed for bliss in Pleasantville, New York, and their idea of a summer vacation is being at the Giants training camp!

Since 1963 (that's 20 years, people), this extraordinary family has made the pilgrimage. Only a veteran like Brad Van Pelt has spent more summers at training camp than the Humphreys. Complete with Giant jerseys and other clothing, the Humphrey's family wash looks like it all came from one place . . . Giants stadium.

The Humphreys continue their devotion during the season, driving a long distance, and always being the first on line when the gates open at 10AM. Their son Dave Jr. has gone from a mild mannered kid who wasn't quite sure of what was going on when he was three years old to the typical teenager who is infected with Giant mania (see inset).

The Humphreys could drive much less to see the Eagles, but David Sr. isn't looking at the gas bills. He, and his family, pictured here in 1973 with Bob Tucker and Joe Walton, are diehards who are driven!

Stadium Staff Favorites

As the Events Manager for Giants Stadium and the Byrne Arena, Bob Castronovo and his staff have come across many strange happenings before, during and after Giants' home games.

He and his ushers, ticket takers and security people have seen it all, and in a conversation this past May, Bob related some of the more oustanding incidents.

"Giants are real drinkers. A lot of beer is sold. One day some 40,000 glasses of beer were purchased, and that doesn't count what the fans drink outside in the parking lot."

"Every game we get some fans who are so intoxicated that they fall asleep during the third or fourth quarter, and we have to wake them up after everyone has left!"

"Once an intoxicated fan fell off his seat onto the playing field and was out cold. It's a problem, but not as bad as some of the really stupid things people do."

"Like the guy who suffered a heart attack during halftime. He refused to be taken to the hospital until the game was over. But for the most part, the fans are good . . . they don't give us much trouble . . . but they do nutty things."

When we beat Dallas in overtime, a dozen guys stripped down to their undershorts in 10 degree weather for at least the whole fourth quarter. We told them they'd probably get frostbite, but they didn't care."

"And, of course, no Giants game would be complete without our 'phantom beauty'. This woman, who is well endowed, stays out of sight until the last two minutes of the game. She then makes a grand entrance, walking down the aisle to the delight of the crowd, the players (we won't tell who) and the TV cameras."

Bob, don't be surprised if you start to get dozens of job applications from our readers!

One fan doesn't feel cold when he watches the Giants.

Remember When . . .

Jim Kearns of Oakland, New Jersey, wrote me a long letter, of his rememberances of special moments in Giants history, starting with his first game in 1938 through the fabulous 50's and the early part of the 1960's. While his focus was on great games, what got to me in this letter was his description of the game on December 14, 1958 against the Cleveland Browns, in which Pat Summerall kicked that 49 yard field goal to win the game. If you can close your eyes after reading this short couple of sentences and try to imagine yourself being there, you'll get a sense of what it was like.

"It was snowing heavily, the flakes falling faster and faster. I can still see that ball, sailing through the uprights, as the Yankee Stadium lights shined on it, ball glistening, shining as it split the goalposts. With yardmarkers covered in snow, players indistinguishable, all that mattered in that frozen moment of time was the path of the ball. With snow blinding our vision and threatening the path of the ball, we hoped and prayed it would make it."

"It made it, and I for one was proud to have been there!"

What a moment as Summerall kicks that winning field goal in the snow.

Travelin' Fans

Don and Marilyn Heiner of Ridgefield Park, New Jersey, are well known, not to the typical Giants fan, but to the airlines, hotels and Giants management, as they attend every single home and away Giants game!

Don has been devoted to the Giants since the late 40's, and became a ticket holder in 1956 when the Giants moved to Yankee Stadium. In 1972, the Heiners scheduled their vacation around a Giants game being played in San Francisco. In 1973 and 1974, they attended all home games and got to more than half the away games: "By this time it had become contagious."

According to Don, "In 1975, we decided to attend all 20 games, home and away, exhibition and regular season. This was in fact accomplished. We have not missed a game since, home or away, exhibition or regular season, plus two playoff games. Our consecutive streak is now 155 games."

If that weren't enough, Don attends the NFL draft, and has been doing so for the past 7 years. They both visit the Giants training camp for several days.

"We both feel a sense of excitement when the schedule of home and away games is announced in April. We plan our vacation schedules—including, if necessary, being away on Labor Day weekend, Christmas and New Year's weekend."

Having been written up in Pro Magazine and interviewed on HBO, the Heiners are a truly unique tribute to Giants mania. One interesting story stands out in their minds.

"During the 1981 season, we were playing in Seattle one weekend and in Atlanta the following weekend. We had two weeks vacation scheduled at that time in San Juan, Puerto Rico. We first flew to Seattle for the first game, and then hopped to Atlanta to New York to San Juan for the first week of the vacation. We stayed in San Juan for a week and flew into Atlanta for the game, leaving most of our clothing and luggage in our hotel room in San Juan. After the game in Atlanta, we flew back to Puerto Rico, enjoyed the rest of our vacation, and then flew home to see the following Sunday's game against the Jets at Giants Stadium."

Don and Marilyn . . . you get the "most miles traveled to see a Giants game award" . . . and you deserve it!

The Stairwell at Gate A

You hear a lot of talk about fans, and their quick regression to violence when things aren't going their way. At the risk of life and limb, I won't name names. On the other hand, Giants fans have been known as sophisticated, smart and certainly non-violent. However, according to Mike (name withheld), our fans do have their moments of barbarism.

During half-time one game, Mike decided, as he puts it, to "avoid the hotdog vendors and an off-key band" and walk around one of the four massive, circular stairways. As Mike reached the perimeter of Stairwell A, "I found hundreds of fellow masochistic followers huddled around the perimeter of the stairwell. There were so many people, hundreds I think, that rail space at all three levels was not to be found."

What did our friend stumble on? Well, I didn't believe it when I read it, but this story has been confirmed. "From there I saw a spectacle only those who participated can truly appreciate. Folks were throwing money down to the bottom of the stairwell. That circular patch of concrete where all the loot landed was nomads land. Anyone attempting to retrieve a small fortune from the arena was promptly pelted from above with everything from beer to spit to tennis balls and game programs. The vocal encouragement was considerable, and as you might imagine, the words were not exactly prim and proper."

We understand that this ritual was short lived, and now security watches over the stairwells to avert such lunacy. In an unique situation where tradition holds together Giants' fans, the fans were denied their own tradition. But, as Mike says, "Some traditions do die. But not the Giants." Did everyone get their quarterback?

That Seat is Mine!

Giants fans get very sentimental about their team, and, amongst other things, their seats at the stadium. It comes as no surprise that when the Giants left Yankee Stadium, many of the fans wanted something to remember the 'good old days' by.

I'm sure Richard Mulvey of Catskill, New York, was one of thousands who came to the last game of the season at Yankee Stadium with more than the usual blankets, cushions, sandwiches and liquid refreshment. As he says, "This day, however, we added a few things like wrenches, screwdrivers, hammers and other tools."

"We had the same seats for years, and we thought of them as ours. We were determined to make those seats our very own momento of the great New York Giants. They weren't any good to anyone, as they were going to do over the stadium."

"I have to confess I saw very little of the game, as I was so busy being a Sunday handyman, trying to unscrew the seats." Having accomplished his task, Richard's visions of a Giants seat in his den was dampened when, late in the 4th quarter, the loudspeaker blared: "Anyone damaging stadium property will be prosecuted." Richard figured it would be a bad example for his 5 children if he was caught stealing the seat. (Ed. Note: some Giants fans would, however, take this risk).

So Richard left Yankee Stadium with a piece of the goal post and his gold plated seat number, which he calls "one of my most treasured possessions."

Every Sunday not an empty seat to be found . . . a true display of loyalty and dedication.

I'll See a Doctor After The Game!

I thought I heard it all until I received this letter in the mail in April of this year. Paul Ruller of Schenectady, New York, relates an experience during a preseason (remember that) game between the Giants and the Steelers last year.

Paul writes, "Being an avid Giants fan, nothing save death (remember that too) was going to deter me from seeing this game, not even the persistent pain in my lower back in the general vicinity of the kidneys. Throughout the four hour drive to the Meadowlands, the pain continued and gradually increased. My wife insisted we turn around and go back home, but I convinced her it was just an upset stomach. So we continued on."

"We arrived at the stadium, and although I still had the pain, the excitement of being at the game took my mind off of it. The pain continued, but this did not stop me from yelling, screaming and jumping up and down."

The game, as you may remember, ended in a 13–10 loss, and Paul doubled over in pain. "We headed back home with me in the back seat in pure agony, my wife burning up the thruway, both of us hoping I would stay alive long enough to get medical attention. We arrived in Schenectady at 3:30AM Sunday morning, where I was admitted to St. Clare's Hospital, and stayed for three days." You can probably guess Paul's kidney stones were removed.

Veterans of kidney stones will sympathize with Paul and what he went through "for the cause." I'd be interested to see if anyone can top that medical story!

Parental Dedication

During one of those years where things weren't going too well, Doreen Fishkin's young boy asked his dad if he could have tickets to one game. Dad said "Sure, take Dallas, it'll be cold then, the Giants will be out of it. I won't want to go."

Our young man was in seventh heaven—he was going to see a Giants game—in person! He thought about nothing but the game as he waited patiently for the big day to arrive. As it happens, the Giants started winning, and that game became crucial. Doreen didn't tell me, but I think dad started begging for the tickets back. I would . . . wouldn't you?

Anyhow, Doreen remembers, "The day of the game the kids got up at the crack of dawn, had a big breakfast, packed their blankets, put on their Giants T-shirts, caps, jersey, jackets, took their lunches and I drove them out to the stadium. I arrived back home to the jangling of the phone . . . it was my son, telling me that he had left the tickets at home!"

"Well, this was at the height of the Christmas shopping season, and I took the tickets, got back in the car, and started to drive out to the stadium. Even with all the traffic, a 40 minute drive, the boys only missed part of the first quarter."

Mrs. Fishkin . . . you win the parent of young Giants fan award!

Emotion and strong vocal chords . . . the trademarks of true Giants fans.

Thou Shalt Not Miss a Play

Rick McDonnell had a very tough decision in the fall of '81. No, it wasn't about his career, his social life, his vacation or taxes. It had to do with a law he and his friends have abided by since the day they became Giants fans: "Thou shalt not miss a play from scrimmage during all regular season and playoff games in which the Giants are involved."

Well, these buddies stuck together through thick and thin, winning and losing, but never broke their pact. Until that fateful Sunday. Rick and his friends stand behind section 113, which is where many of the Giants wives and families sit. Due to the longevity of Joe Danelo's career, his wife had become one of the few faces the boys recognized every year.

Rick continues: "It was the middle of the third quarter, and the Giants were in the midst of a scoring drive, when we noticed Mrs. Danelo taking her young daughter to the ladies room . . . a popular spot on this cold day. As I lifted my head after the next play, my eye was caught by a young boy a few rows down, looking my way, a tear in his eye, his legs pressed together, hands in his pockets, obviously in pain. The two empty seats next to him led to one conclusion: this was Joe Danelo's son, who was left by his lonesome and in desperate need of emptying a full bladder."

Well, this is one of those decisions that try men's souls. Rick had two choices—keep to his pact and ignore little Joe, or escort him to the men's room and risk living in sin forever. Rick made his decision . . .

"I quickly signaled to the boy to meet me at the top of the aisle. He grabbed my hand and we trotted into the men's room. Once inside, I informed everyone of the situation—and the little fella went right to the head of the line. Upon our return, a relieved Mrs. Danelo thanked me. As I walked up to join my friends, I wondered how badly I would be raked over the coals. To this day, my friends never said a word . . . I guess you know what true friends are all about."

Travel Plans

Stu Landau writes us with two short stories, which he titles "What I have done for the 'cause'." Since both of his stories involve seeing the games from great distances, I've titled it 'Travel Plans.'

Stu remembers back to 1970 when the Giants took on the Jets in regular season play. It was Namath versus Tarketon, but Stu was at a Bar Mitzvah. He continues: "I could not stand the pressure any longer, so I sneak out. I walk a mile and find a little bar in Queens. There are Giants fans on one side of the bar, and Jets fans on the other. Two hours later I return to my wife. She doesn't talk to me for a week." Ed. Note: about average, Stu.

Stu, who lives in Londonderry, New Hampshire (way, way up there) goes to all the Giants home games. It's 250 miles, or five hours by car. Once he was on a four month assignment in Littleton, near the Canadian border (yes, people do live up there!). As he says, "375 miles and almost 8 hours".

The Friday before the Philadelphia game, "I took off early and called my wife. I told her to be at the door with the kids and suitcases at 12 noon. I left Littleton at 9:30, picked up my family at noon, and was down in NJ at 5PM, and ready for the next day's game!"

If I had a penny for every gallon of gas used to get to a Giants game . . .

Everybody prays for the Giants in different ways . . . this fan makes no bones about it!

Forget the Celebration, The Giants Are Playing Tomorrow!

One of General Manager George Young's favorite stories happened when he was playing football at Bucknell. His roomate, from North Bergen, was a die hard Giants fan.

Bucknell went undefeated that year, and, according to George, "Everyone went out to celebrate after the final game. But my friend wasn't interested in spending Saturday night enjoying our triumphant season."

"He and I got into his '48 Chevy and drove over the Poconos (they didn't have Route 80 then), through New Jersey to the Polo Grounds to watch the Giants play Cleveland the next day!"

It's not a hard scene to picture: the entire campus out getting loaded into the wee hours, and George and his buddy creeping along the back roads in the middle of the night. For George's buddy, it was part of being a die-hard fan. For George, it was a premonition!

An upper deck group of fans create a Giant sized pennant!

Great View!

Living on the Grand Concourse in the Bronx in the 1960's, Frank Roberts was a stone's throw from Yankee Stadium. Frank's buddy lived in a 6 story apartment house just one block from the ballpark.

Armed with a portable radio and binoculars, they trekked up to the roof every Sunday where they had a bird's eye view of the Giants. They could see just about all the field, and had a nice angle to watch the game.

Frank remembers one game, where Y.A. Tittle completed 5 or 6 TD passes, most to Del Shofner, in a game against the Redskins. He picks it up here, "After the game, hundreds of fans were celebrating on the subway elevated platform, which we could see from our rooftop perch. The crowd became unusually large due to a train delay, and the platform began to sway as the people got more and more unruly. It looked like it would collapse!"

I can picture it now . . . the sweet smells of Sunday dinners wafting up to the roof as Frank and his friends watched the Giants in a cool, light breeze. Would I have loved to be there . . .

All rise . . . as the Giants break a long gainer.

Say a Little Prayer For Us

The Berger family of Whitestone, New York, travel to many away Giants games. Their son, who is in college and manages the football teams, still finds time to see the Giants at home, and in Philadelphia and Washington.

Two years ago, the family drove to Philadelphia in their brand new car, with vanity license plates reading "Giants". According to the Bergers, "We knew the Philly fans were rough, and we wondered about our defenseless new car with the Giants plates, sitting like a duck in the hostile parking lot. At the game was a nun, Sister Caroline, a Giants fan, who sat with the Giants contingent. Although we are not of her faith, we snuggled close and prayed that the Giants would win, and our car would make it safely out of the parking lot" (Ed. Note: probably in that order).

Well, the Giants did win and the Bergers made it home without a scratch. Now let's all pray for a Super Bowl appearance this year!

Hands high, everyone celebrates another Giants TD.

Keeping Warm . . .

At Yankee Stadium, many people in the stands kept warm on a cold wintry day by lighting small fires in the upper deck. Of course, those days are gone, but one fan wrote in with a 'recipe' of her own for beating those cold wintry nights.

She writes, "Bring lots of newspaper and put it under your feet. That will provide insulation against the cold cement and your feet will stay warm. Make hot wine in the morning and keep it in a thermos. Bring hot steaming cocoa for the kids."

That sounds great, Joan Raab! But, she writes, "My husband doesn't care about the cold. Even when it's zero degrees, he'll still be drinking beer!"

CHAPTER 5

Don't disturb me, I'm watching the game!

Parking Permitted
1–4PM Sundays

Not all of us are blessed with crystal clear TV reception or static free radio broadcasts of Giants games. Among those that weren't were Lou and Sue Foster, now of Pawling, New York, but once from the wilderness of New Hampshire.

Sue wrote us with this tale of die-hardedness. "We've done many things to give the games our undivided attention, but I guess the strangest was when my husband was attending the University of New Hampshire. We did a lot of pre-season research and found only one location in the 'area' where radio reception was statical at best, but audible. So every Sunday afternoon—all season long—through all kinds of weather—we would drive 20 miles and park on the overpass at the Seabrook Exit of Interstate 95 for three hours!"

Now that the Fosters get the games on TV, those days of overpasses are past . . . or, we wonder, have they discovered other things to do in a parked car!?

Jolly Good Show!

I received a letter back in March of this year, postmarked England. It was from a Mr. Bev Wills, and he wrote, "Being an Englishman, and also a resident in Great Britain, my main problem is catching Giants games at all."

"Fortunately the Giants are covered regularly on the Armed Forces Radio and Television Service, which is broadcast via satellite to Europe, and gives live radio coverage of games. Because of the difference in time zones, this can lead to listening at some anti-social hours."

"I dread West Coast road games. For example, the play-off contest against the 49ers finished at 2AM Monday morning. These games involve me going to bed with the earplug in the radio so as not to disturb my wife, but I do have great trouble restraining my shouts of triumph when the Giants score a TD."

"However, the biggest threat to domestic bliss comes if the Giants are featured in a Monday night game (also broadcast live). These matches (Ed: how cute!) start at 2AM Tuesday morning, and to tune in involves going to bed early and setting the alarm. Needless to say, I would do that for Giants games only!"

I'm sure there are hundreds of fellow Britons, as well as fans around the globe who put sleep behind the Giants . . . to these people, wherever they may reside . . . you're wonderful!

Super Reverend!

The Reverend Forrest Shue, Sr. of Bloomsbury, New Jersey (heart of Eagle country) is a super Giants fan. In addition to being a man of the cloth, he is a man of the jersey, Giants jerseys that is.

His wife, Joy, sent me a very funny letter back in March of this year. Near the end, she wrote "I've tried to keep this letter about him secret, as a surprise. I'm sure if you mention his name and his antics in your book, you would be assured a place in heaven!"

Well, Reverend, here it is . . . just send me my ticket!

All kidding aside, Reverend Shue is an unbelievable Giants fan. Ever wonder what Church leaders wear under their vestments? I don't know about others, but this one wears a Giants T-shirt! At home, he wears a Giants hat!

Two years ago, our Reverend found it difficult concluding Sunday services and being home in time for the one o'clock kickoff. So he changed (with much difficulty) the starting time of the service from 11 to 10AM.

Sunday dinner revolves around the game, which, according to Joy, "we usually end up eating at halftime. So much for long dinners with plenty of family conversation. 20 minutes is the limit."

Reverend Shue also has a problem watching the games on TV. Channel 2's reception isn't that great, so much time and money has been spent in trying to find the right antenna combination! Joy says, "He still sits in front of a snowy television screen, insisting he can actually see what's going on." That must be a side benefit of being in the service of the Lord.

Part of Reverend Shue's collection of Giants memorabilia.

He travels 20 miles every Monday morning to get the Star Ledger for its coverage of the Giants games. He gets the Giants highlight films, and has a Friday night viewing for those interested. "He sets up our yard as an outdoor theater with his Giants Museum on display. Every article of Giants memorabilia he owns is dragged outdoors on tables, under a spotlight, for everyone to see. People go on vacation and bring him souvenirs for his collection!"

"We own a blue and white van, and recently it has been graced with the Giants logo on the back. I could go on forever about my zany husband, and how he rushes me out of Church on my cousins' wedding day to sit in the car and hear the score. After all, who in their right mind gets married on Sunday anyway?"

Somehow with a fan like the Reverend Shue out there, you get the feeling that someday we'll all benefit from the special connections he has. Let's hope it's this year!

Fine Tuning . . .

You'd be surprised how many people in Pennsylvania are die-hard Giants fans. Eric Lund, who used to live in Slatington, is one example.

Undaunted by the local cable TV company which didn't receive Channel 2 from New York, Eric decided if he was going to watch Giants games, he'd have to do it himself.

He purchased a $100 antenna and installed it on his roof. According to Eric, the distance between Slatington and New York made for a "very weak and snowy picture."

Not about to move, but also not about to be deprived of Giants football, Eric and his wife Patty spent Sunday afternoons performing the same ritual: "Twenty minutes before the pre-game show I would go up on the roof and start turning the antenna. Patty, stationed at the tuner on the TV, would yell out to me when the reception was best. As you might imagine, this was a pain in the neck on rainy days, and slightly dangerous in thunder and lightning storms. The picture was never very clear, and I had to turn off all the lights and pull down all the shades in the room just to see what was going on."

Now the Lunds live in New Hampshire, and get the Giants games through the Boston station. I suspect, however, that two years of peering at snow-laden TV screens has made our 28 year old fan very, very nearsighted. But, when it comes to the Giants, any illness is worth it . . . right?

Role Reversal

In the numerous conversations I've had researching this book, I've come across many wives of Giants fans who have joined their husbands in their fanatacism rather than fighting it. But none to the extreme of Bert Rosenkrantz's wife. She had been a football widow for many years, and went through the typical wonderment that wives do who don't understand this craziness.

Well, Bert finally wrangled two tickets to a game, and took his wife along. Throughout the game, he explained what was happening on the field, the rules and so forth. A quick education about the game and the Giants.

Bert was as surprised as I was: "It didn't take too long before she was bugging me to get season tickets. Fortunately, we were able to buy a season's worth of tickets from a friend. By the third or fourth game, my wife knew where the players graduated from, who traded them and that sort of stuff. If the weather was threatening, she would insist we go, rain or shine."

The last home game of that season was on a snowy Sunday. A couple of inches had fallen the night before and it was windy. "My wife insisted (as wives sometimes do) that we go to the game being that next year we wouldn't have season tickets anymore. We bundled up, took all the blankets, hot coffee and other stimulants."

"When I hit the slippery roads, covered with ice, I was furious. I assumed she would see how bad the driving was and we'd turn back. Heck, I love the Giants, but I prefer to live a nice long life. Anyhow, we drove about three miles in 45 minutes and were skidding all over the road. I just refused to continue—after all, it was only a game."

Well, Bert won out and turned around and drove home. But he really didn't win, for he got the cold treatment from his spouse for three solid days. The scene was worse when they got home: "Even before she took off her coat, she turned on the TV . . . to show me that there were indeed people who went, and that we could have made it if I had tried."

"During the season, she is the one glued to the set, and I can make no plans for a Monday night (it interferes with HER game), and everything revolves around the game." Bert makes signs for a living, and one should be made for him: 'Let's hear it for women's Giants fans!'

Long Distance Love Affair

Giants fans are scattered all over the country, and one such fan, a car dealer from San Diego, was a die-hard who never missed a game when he lived on the east coast.

Crazy Louie, as he's come to be known, solved this problem, with the usual ingenuity that has become the trademark of Giants football fans.

His mom lived in Brooklyn, so every Sunday, he would call her up, and she'd place the receiver of the phone next to a radio playing the game. For three hours, he sit listening to the game over the phone.

I called Ma Bell and found the average cost for a three hour call between San Diego and Brooklyn would run about $36.00 plus tax. Not exactly my best way to spend money, but if I lived on the West Coast, I'd probably do the same.

Let's go to the Videotape . . .
OR
The Art of Betamaxing Giants Victories!

When the Giants win, part of the fun is watching the highlights, for everyone whoops up on a Giant victory. Somehow, our touchdowns look better and sweeter than everyone else's and watching them over and over and over and over makes that feeling even better.

I go crazy to get the highlights on my Betamax when the Giants win. In fact, if you time it right, you can get the same highlights from 4 or 5 different TV stations. I tape them all, even with the same play repeated 5 times! Then I've got 10 minutes of pure Giant supremacy, which I watch over and over. I feel like a little kid eating candy at Halloween . . . get glutted now because October 31st doesn't come for another year.

To Heck With That Job!

This amusing story comes from 21 year old Bart Fellin of Middlesex, NJ who worked part time at a liquor store on Sundays. He spent most of his time stacking beer inside one of the large, and very very cold, refrigerators.

Knowing that he was going to miss Giants football, he purchased a radio that would work inside the metal refrigerator. For the first couple of weeks, it worked fine, Bart listening to the game while stacking beer. The coldness of the refrigerator even made him feel as if he was at Giants Stadium in the dead of winter.

But, according to Bart, that wasn't good enough. "Listening to the game was all right, but nothing compared to seeing the game. So I quit the job!"

Poor Bart. Little did he know that the NFL would go on strike the next week! Nor did he get his job at the liquor store back. But after a couple of months, we heard he now works as a salesman in a popular department store . . . selling TV's! He could be there forever!

Change My Work Schedule!

Ed Ball of Hillside, New Jersey simply will not work any Sunday the Giants play at home. Where he works, 10 employees split up weekend shifts, so Ed has to work every 4th or 5th Sunday.

His supervisor knows Ed won't work if there is a home game that Sunday, and he grants Ed's wishes. What's more interesting than that is Ed's philosophy on the whole deal: "Hey, if someone can ask the supervisor for a Saturday or Sunday off for a wedding, funeral or such, then why can't I use my days for Giants games?"

Let's hear it for flextime!

Honeymoon Humdinger!

Jack Goellner of Erie, Pennsylvania, is a die-hard Giants fan. He has autographed pictures, souvenirs, and dresses in a Giants jersey when watching the game, is a member of the Erie Giants fan club, subscribes to Inside Football, has rented motel rooms to watch games on Cable, and so forth. Of course, Jack is no different in that respect from thousands of us. But he pulled a doosy on his first honeymoon.

"In 1972, we were on our honeymoon, traveling through upstate New York. On Sunday morning before we left the motel, my wife stopped in a drugstore. I immediately seized the opportunity to check a TV Guide, and sure enough, the Giants were scheduled to play the 49ers on Channel 10. I asked the clerk if Channel 10 was received throughout the area, and she assured me it was. We got on the road about noon, heading for Whiteface Mountain.''

We interrupt this tale to place it in perspective. Here's this young man, just married, heading on a honeymoon adventure in an area that makes you forget about civilization. Back to the story.

"About 12:30 I started complaining about pains in my back, so much that my wife took over the driving. By 12:45 I was faking agony, and told her we'd have to get a motel room where I could lie down. She couldn't believe it, but I convinced her and we found a little out of the way motel.''

We interrupt this tale again to point out that most people would think our young man faked agony to get to a motel for other reasons, though you'll see differently. Back to the story.

"Before I checked in at the desk, I asked if they got Channel 10. As if knowing, the proprietor said 'Giants fan, huh? Take Room 4. It's got the best TV'. I thanked him and hurried to my room, where I moaned as I got into bed. Instead of just asking my wife to turn on the TV, I asked her to turn on Channel 10. When she saw the game she really blew up. That's the end of the story, and also the beginning of the end of that marriage.''

Today Jack is happily married, and his second wife loves football and the Giants. We don't expect any more shenanigans from you, Jack!

Nuptial Signal Calling

While at the wedding of her cousin during the 1981 season, Joan Bowen of Irvington, New Jersey, noticed something odd.

From the minute the procession started to the groom's exit under a shower of rice, his best man kept whispering something in the groom's ear. Everyone must have thought the best man was coaching a nervous husband-to-be, but Joan and her husband "weren't surprised when we found out the best man had a portable radio in his pocket and he was keeping the groom abreast of how the Giants were faring in their game with the Philadelphia Eagles.''

All's well that ends well . . . Joan's cousin is still happily married, and, of course, the Giants won a thriller over Philly.

Delay Of Birth . . .
No Penalty!

Allan Berman of Irvington, New Jersey, was an expectant father in December of 1981 . . . in more ways than one.

"During the afternoon of December 27th," he writes, "both my wife and the Giants were in labor. My wife was in the process of giving birth to our son, and the Giants were laboring to eliminate the Eagles from the NFL playoffs."

"Fortunately, the expectant fathers' lounge was right across the corridor from my wife's room, so I ran back and forth between her room and the TV in the lounge, being with her during time outs and incomplete passes." So fast were Allan's dashes to and fro that doctors and nurses stayed clear of this crazed fan and father-to-be.

Fortunately, "the obstetrician was a Giant fan, and my wife was very understanding. Since the delivery was to be a Caesarian, and the doctors wanted to see the end of the game, my wife called her own little delay of birth. She said we should all watch the game, and then come and deliver Joshua. Which we did!"

Two awards are due here: for Joshua's mom, the "most understanding moment for a football fan's wife" award, and for the obstetricians, the "doctors make good Giants fans too" award.

Food For Thought

Patti Magee, a reporter for the Register-Star (Hudson, NY) sent us two articles she wrote about Robert Ward III and his family, a bunch of die-hard Giants fans.

Like many of us, Robert and his son never miss a Giants game, approach each and every play with the same feelings of anxiety and can't handle life without the red, white and blue team from the Meadowlands.

Only Robert takes things in another direction—he creates special meals for game day, which he makes and eats during the game! His secret, according to Patti, is "We don't schedule meals around football games. We schedule them through the games."

With recipes having names like 'Beans That Hot The Tongue' and 'Texas Hot Weiner Sauce' you can guess what Robert has a lot of on hand—beer. Whatever he's cooking, it's got to go well with beer.

Now Robert, with the kind assistance of Patti and her newspaper, are willing to share one of Robert's recipes with all of us Giants fans. Try 'Applesauce Meatballs' next time the Giants play.

APPLESAUCE MEATBALLS

3–4 lbs. ground beef
1–4 lbs. bulk sausage
1–2 cup fine bread crumbs
1 egg
1 cup applesauce
2 tbsp. grated onion
1 tsp. salt
1–8 oz. can tomato sauce

Combine all ingredients except tomato sauce. Mix lightly and form into one-inch footballs. Brown in electric frying pan in hot vegetable oil. Drain off fat. Add tomato sauce. Cover and cook at 325 degrees for one hour. Serve only when Giants have the ball!

Revolving Door

According to Jim (last name witheld upon request) of Staten Island, New York, his experience as a Giants fan has always been great fun, at times challenging, and sometimes, as we will see, dangerous to his employment.

Working as a dietary worker at a local hospital, Jim had to work every other weekend, and during football season, we all know what that meant . . . no Giants games.

Jim, like many of us, had two choices: "First, I could call in sick every other weekend, or bring a radio to work with me. I chose the second idea."

"My first problem was reception inside the hospital, which was terrible. Great plays were reduced to static. My second problem was my supervisor, who told me to leave my radio at home. However, he didn't say anything about a transistor radio, which I hooked up with wires under my shirt and a nifty ear plug."

Unfortunately, Jim's transistor radio didn't improve the reception of the game. His final plan: parking illegally by the loading dock, Jim would run outside to catch snatches of the game in his car. According to him, "I never missed the final two minutes of the second or fourth quarters."

When the Giants played Dallas, Jim kept going in and out, from the warmth of the kitchen, out into a cold, rainy November day. For the last series of the game, Jim ran out into the car, and found his supervisor and friend sitting there, listening to the game! Jim was warned again, but said "OK, write me up, but I'm not going to miss the final four minutes of this game!"

Well, Jim didn't miss the rest of that 38–35 thriller, and for the last four minutes, the three of them (Jim, his friend and his supervisor) sat in the car and cheered, laughed and clapped as the Giants went on to shock the Cowboys.

We hear from informed sources inside the hospital that the entrance to the loading dock now has an iron gate which can only be opened electronically, that Jim's supervisor was transferred to Oklahoma, and that Jim has a pocket TV which he keeps inside the microwave oven!

Ballet and Football . . . Bravo!

One of our fans who wishes to remain anonymous recently attended the ballet on a Sunday afternoon. Of course, the Giants were playing a crucial game, and both kickoff and opening were to coincide.

Not willing to give up the Giants, our fan recalls that day. "We were at the famous Brooklyn Academy of Music . . . my wife and I, my cousins and my little radio with earphones."

"It really was the best of both worlds. The dancing in the ballet was not that bad . . . in fact, it was pretty good. But I didn't hear the music. It was a great game, and by some coincidence, highlights in the ballet seemed to coincide with touchdowns and field goals by the Giants."

"The only problem occurred when my cousin tried to take my coat, which concealed my radio, and put it with the others on an empty seat. We had a little tug of war. But since the Giants won that day, nothing, not even the stifling heat, the crowds or even the lack of a TV bothered me. As the ballet dancers soared, so did I."

Thank Heavens For Sportsphone!

I don't know what thousands of Giants fans would do without Sportsphone. If you were to look at the telephone bill of Giants fans, the biggest item during any given Sunday would have to be the Sportsphone.

When we just can't get to a TV or radio during the game, Sportsphone gives many of us play by play! I was at my cousin's wedding, and couldn't sneak in a radio . . . didn't want to take chances of getting caught! True blue fans would accuse me of chickening out, but I just couldn't risk it. Anyhow, I did the next best thing . . . stocked up on dimes and quarters and made sure there was a phone in the reception hall.

I called Sportsphone every 10 minutes and relayed the latest scores to the other Giant faithfuls at the affair. Every time I entered the room, two thoughts were in the people's minds: those who didn't know what I was doing thought I had the runs. Those who knew what was going on were looking for any sign—thumbs up, a smile, a grin—to let them know what was happening to their beloved team. Without Sportsphone, I just don't know how I could have made it through the wedding!

Giant Slopes!

Stuart Wolff of Fresh Meadows, New York, had a dilemna last year. On the same day the Giants were scheduled to play the Eagles, Stu had an invitation to go skiing.

Being a die-hard Giants fan, Stu never misses a game. But being an avid skier, he wanted to hit the slopes.

Well, for every problem, there is a Giant solution—Stu brought his Walkman radio with headphones hid under his skiing cap. So all day long, while hurtling down the slopes, he heard every play of the game! Of course, the Giants won, making it a truly memorable afternoon.

However, I wonder if Mr. Wolff lost control at critical points during the game. Reliable sources credit broken bones, bruises and grogginess after the game due to bumping into stationary objects while skiing. Stu, next time do your skiing during halftime, time outs and commercials.

The Forecast is for Rain . . .

Charles Nash Jr. of Middlesex, New Jersey, like so many others, had to attend a wedding on a Sunday afternoon. Being poor, 24 and not a season ticket holder, Charlie never-the-less never misses a play.

His wife had previously purchased Charlie a portable TV, which he watches while working at his hot dog stand. After the ceremony, which was thoughtfully timed to end just before 1 o'clock, "my wife held the television on her lap as I drove to the country club for the reception. Since reception was poor, I also had the radio on."

"We arrived at the club, I walked my wife in and grabbed a couple of drinks, and went back to the car to watch the game. It was close (against Dallas, 1980) and the Blue Wall was fired up."

"Because of the rain, reception inside the car was nonexistent, and in order to see, I had to stand outside the car, with the television on the roof—in the rain!"

Well, we all know what happened to Charlie's suit that

day, but it was worth it. The Giants beat Dallas. Ironically, in the country club civilized Giants fans were watching the game in another room, which Charlie, of course, didn't know about. His feeling on being left out in the rain: "I did not care." Way to go, Charlie!

Happy Anniversary!

It seems as if preseason games and anniversaries, weddings, births or any other special occasions just don't mix, or at least, create problems for die-hards.

One young man, Robert Mahar, writes: "I remember taking my wife out for dinner this past summer on our anniversary. After dinner, I decided it would be nice to go bar hopping. I didn't tell my wife the reason for going from bar to bar—the local radio station was broadcasting a preseason Giants game live. I made sure the bars were spaced out nicely, and tuned one ear to the radio and the other to my wife!"

Ed. Note: Giants fans must be born with the ability to listen to the game and a spouse at the same time.

Thou Shalt Watch Giants Games!

Bob Murphy of Smithtown, New York, has followed the Giants from the Polo Grounds to Giants Stadium, with Yankee Stadium and New Haven in between. Nothing, however, can top the seat he had for the 1961 season.

"In August of 1961, I entered my third year of study for the priesthood. This was to be a year spent in prayer, silence, penance and manual labor, completely removed from the noise and hub-bub of the outside world, at a novitate in Essex, New York."

Our priest-to-be was doing OK until the second Sunday in September . . . football season. "I discovered that the novice masters' house, with the big antenna sitting on it, was the gathering place for the local priests to watch—of all things—my Giants."

"Before the first quarter ended, I discovered a crawl space beneath the house, about three feet high and four feet wide, which went directly under the TV room. For the next 14 weeks, I did three hours of penance in that crawl space! Every Sunday I listened to the game—unable to move, and worse, unable to cheer as Y.A. Title took the Giants to the Eastern Conference Championship with a 10–3–1 record."

Today, as Bob passes the luxury boxes with sofas, bars, waiters, and other amenites of the good life, our dauntless and silent fan wonders: "How could anyone enjoy a Giant game in such luxurious surroundings?" I agree!

Medal of Honor!

I received hundreds of letters in researching this project, all from self-admitted Giant maniacs. This one, from Robert Drossman of Nesconset, New York, starts off "Here is one story from a crazy!" Self admitted crazies, that's what we all are!

Robert continues, "In the late 1960's I was in the National Guard, and we had week-end meetings. In order not to miss any games, I used to make up the Sunday meetings by going to four additional week-day meetings. During a span when the Giants had four straight home games, I had to spend every evening of the week playing soldier at my armory in order to see us lose on Sunday."

Ed. note: Maybe, Robert, you picked the wrong year to be in the Guard. Now, at least, we're winning, so that your weekly service might have been more worthwhile! But anyway, here's to good service!

A Little Birdie Told Me . . .

Lee Fernandes of Roselle, New Jersey and his friends root for the Giants just like the rest of us . . . sitting in front of the TV, whooping it up, being in a frenzy. With one exception.

Their pet "Snowflake" also roots for the red and blue. Trained to say "Go Giants Go" by Lee's wife, their Australian parakeet perches on Lee's shoulder and excitedly takes part in the action! His friends didn't believe it until they saw it.

Shopper's Paradise!

You know how they have those regular announcements in supermarkets and department stores that run "Shoppers, during the next hour, you can save an additional 25 cents on pantyhose . . . ?" This story concerns some innovative loudspeaker programming developed by Richard Carbone of Verplanck (where's that), New York. When managing one of their chain stores, Richard, being a die hard Giants fan, would sometimes get carried away. So much carried away that instead of Campbell's soup or Alpo on sale, customers would hear play by play Giants fan in the store at the time of the game. (see note below) He loved it. But other customers (see second note below) didn't and complained. Their short-sightedness and lack of consideration for true fans cost Richard his job. What a damn shame!

Note #1: A true Giants fan wouldn't be shopping during the game, unless it was an extreme emergency, in which case he'd have a radio with him.

Note #2: How can people be so inconsiderate and stupid. Who cares how much pomegranites or two day old bread costs?

CHAPTER 6

Great moments in Giants fan history!

Sweet Recollections . . .

By Vinny DiTrani
The Bergen Record

Vinny DiTrani has been covering the Giants for that fabulously colorful newspaper in Bergen County, The Record. In this piece, however, he takes us back to when he himself was a fan.

In this day of sold-out Giants stadium and a waiting list a half-mile long, it's somewhat difficult to imagine that 25 years ago, 50 cents and a high school ID card could get you a seat in the bleachers on the 40-yard line at Yankee Stadium.

That was the case when myself and other high school aged Giants fans would gather at the bus stop in suburban Emerson, NJ on Sunday mornings, looking for transportation into the city. A stop at the old bus terminal at 168th Street, and a subway ride with a changeover at 145th usually would get us to the Stadium at around 10AM.

Since these were the days before the television takeover, the kickoff was not until 2PM, making for four long hours to kill. But an early arrival was essential to get near the front of the line and a chance at those seats near the Yankee bullpen, which lined up at about the 40.

Killing those hours, especially in the later weeks of the season, often included a game of kick-the-cup soccer, played in the darker confines underneath the bleachers, with one or two of the group left behind to "save the seats" in the first come, first serve open bleacher area. The memories didn't end with the final whistle, either. After each game a portion of the group, which always included myself, Brian "Crash" Corrigan and Bob "Sunshine" Henry, gathered outside the players' entrance. The first time we met, the guard on duty informed us we couldn't stand around the door, that we had to go across the street and beyond the police barriers.

"Oh, it's okay," I informed the guard. "We're friends of Andy Robustelli's sons and he told us to wait here." Then, when Robustelli exited, we trotted off behind him, like we

61

belonged. After a while, the guard got to know us and leaving with Andy wasn't necessary anymore.

In 1961 the Giants had a halfback named Joe Wells from Clemson, who played enough not to be a nobody but who was not easily recognizable to the average fan. So we decided that Crash, who had a beard that belied his tender age of 16, would become Joel Wells after games.

Crash would walk from the area near the exit with the rest of us yelling "Hey, there goes Joe Wells." By the end of the season, Crash had inked more Joel Wells autographs than Joel Wells did himself!

And then there was Jungle Jamie, one of the famous camp hangers of all time, whose trademarks were a safari hat and a cowboy hat, each covered by autographs of famous athletes. We met Jamie one day as we stood by the door, waiting for good ol' Andy to come out. He was telling someone how he knew all the players, and we figured he was a phony.

Then out came the late Phil King. "Hey Phil, remember that dollar you owe me?" cried Jamie. King stopped, took out his wallet, and gave Jamie a dollar.

Several other players acknowledged Jamie, so Crash and I decided to check out this character. We found out he was employed as defensive back Dick Lynch's valet!

Soon he had talked us into attending a Saturday practice session at Yankee Stadium prior to a late-season game with the Browns. Then, he said, he would help us get sideline passes from Lynch so we could stand among the Giants during the game.

We met Jamie at his home, which was the back room of a bar down around Herald Square, and subwayed up to the Stadium. After lunch at the automat, we walked towards the ballpark. "I'm going up to see some of the Browns at their hotel; just tell the guard you're friends of Dick Lynch and he'll let you in," Jamie told us.

Surprisingly, the guard did let us in, and even directed us down to the field. It was an experience—the sound of Don Chandler's punts echoing throughout the empty stadium; the sight of Darrell Dess rejoicing after he was "demoted" off the kickoff team. After watching the light practice session, we tried to rejoin Jamie at the Browns' hotel. But he was nowhere to be found.

The fact that the two of us were going to be on the sidelines that Sunday made for great bragging to our envious friends. We met Jamie in front of the players' entrance, but as the Giants arrived, Lynch whisked him through the door before Jamie could introduce us.

We were stranded. We raced around to the bleacher entrance. Luckily, an ice storm the night before had kept down the crowd somewhat, and we still could purchase our prized 50 cent seats. Unfortunately, we wound up sitting next to most of the guys we told to look for us on the field.

After the game we once again met Jamie, who apologized: "They're cracking down on sideline passes," he explained. "I was lucky to get in myself." Jamie was around for several seasons before disappearing. Last time I saw him was after an exhibition game in Seattle in the mid-70's. He still was hanging around football teams, though he no longer wore his great hats.

Look, Up In The Sky . . .

This is the story of two protests, both coming out of the frustrations felt by die-hard fans. The "Ticket Burning" was the result of "the fumble" and a general dissatisfaction of recent Giant foibles, and the "Sign From the Sky" was the result of suffering through over 15 years of poor quality football. Both stories illustrate the extent people will go for the sake of their team. They simply are amazing.

The Burning

Sounds like the title of a horror movie or Stephen King book, but it was an expression of frustration felt during the height of the Giants misfortunes. According to The Star Ledger's report, "Claiming they were acting 'in memory of Giants teams of the past' a small group of irate fans burned some 100 tickets outside Giants Stadium prior to the start of the game."

According to Ron Freiman and Gene McNevins of New Jersey, the protest was intended to send a message to the Giants management, to let them know the fans were not happy with the way the team was being handled.

Gene McNevins and Ron Freiman lead the protest. Inset: the flame symbolizes the fans' dedication and love for the team.

To Gene McNevins; a real GIANTS FAN
Bil

Canfield cartoon in the Star-Ledger commemorating the burning.

As protests go, this one made the news media, and probably was the beginning of the end of the miserable years. Coupled with the sign episode, the two protests had to have some impact.

The Sign

In 1978, a group of fans created protest which was visible to thousands and demonstrated, once again, the determination of genuine true-blue fans.

Dave Anderson, in his column for The New York Times the day after, wrote the following:

"With more love than hate, as if rehearsing a polite scolding of an old relative, the members of the Giants Fans Committee passed out mimeographed sheets yesterday at Giants stadium that announced: 'On or about 1:30PM, there will be a sign from the sky—We've Had Enough—if you feel we Giant Fans have suffered long enough, pass this along the aisle to other Die Hard Giant Fans and join in a unison chant of 'We've Had Enough'. We have been the most supportive, loyal fans in the world. Maybe if we all raise our voices, our message will reach management. We cannot wait another 15 years for a championship!'"

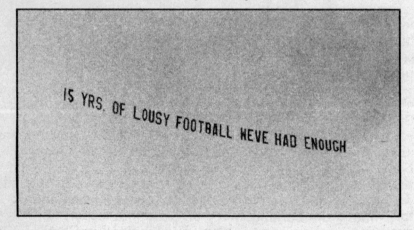

Look, up in the sky . . .

"The sign from the sky was about an hour late and when it fluttered by, attached to a small plane, it read '15 Years of Lousy Football . . . We've Had Enough'. Moments later the chant began from many in the chilled gathering of 52,226, 'We've had enough . . . we've had enough . . . we've had enough.'"

In nearby Clifton three hours before game time, 95 loyalists, almost all adults, appeared at a cost of $3 each to cover the banquet room rental at The Ramada Inn, coffee, orange juice and danish for the Giants fans. The committee's first convention chairman, Morris Speilberg, displayed a handwritten letter from Wellington Mara, prompted by Spielberg's recent advertisement in the Star Ledger. 'If you would care to forward to us the replies that you get,' Mara wrote, 'I would like to try to answer them.'"

"Peter Valentine then outlined four major issues which the committee would seek action on. Fans had suggestions for getting new playbooks and a new coach. One fan said 'We don't settle for 17 points'. The Giants had scored 17 points in each of three consecutive losses; yesterday they scored 17 and won. But for the Giants now, it's not whether you win or lose, it's whether you listen to the fans."

Apparently Mara and company did listen, for the year following the sign things started to change. Now, four years later, we've been selected to be on Monday night football and see the light at the end of the tunnel. But not without some hardships and protests. As Anderson writes in a followup column in 1981: "They weren't terrorists. They hadn't hijacked the plane, merely rented it. And that small plane didn't have any explosives, only a sign fluttering behind it. But that protest by a group of Giants fans three years ago was explosive enough to contribute to the changes that now have the Giants only two victories from Super Bowl XVI."

From the point of view of the many fans who simply heard about these protests, it was "something good that somebody finally did". For those that went out and burned their tickets, and for those that organized the "sign in the sky" it was something most people don't do very often: stand up for what you believe in. That's an important lesson for everyone . . . let's hope it never repeats itself in Giants stadium!

P.S. We heard, just at presstime, from the originator of another sign-from-the sky, this one which flew over in 1980. Martin Wall's message read "We Need These Giants Like Custer Needed More Indians." I wonder how many more planes never made it off the ground during that period. But, with a contender in sight, I think the planes will be silent for a long time to come.

A Short Story . . . And a Song

A mild-mannered lawyer Monday through Friday, my brother becomes a crazed Giants fan on weekends and Monday nights. So I decided to put his talents to work and asked him to write a short story for this book. It came out so good that I coerced him into writing a song. I think you'll enjoy both.

The Year

By Howard Brechner

It was a Saturday night in September and while party crowds attacked the city, one man nervously turned off the 10 o'clock news at 10:20.

He ambled over to his large brass bed, called weakly good night to his wife, stubbed all the toes on his left foot, and hopped angrily into the bathroom in pain. Rubbing his foot, he stared into the medicine cabinet mirror and scrutinized the face gazing back.

He wished it were someone else, for what he had to do the next day was a task perhaps left for better men.

Soon it was 11:30 and the warrior was still wide awake, tossing wearily. By 12, the sheets were soaked, but by twenty to one, the tired soul finally fell into an uneasy, foggy slumber.

68

Lights danced before his eyes and wild images whizzed by. Suddenly, there were clouds and angels everywhere. It was apparent that this was Heaven and he was being offered the choice of two doors:

1, before which was placed a pair of red, white and blue cleats, and

2, before which lay an olive-colored sword with a fierce eagle emblazoned on its shaft.

The sweet looking cherubic angels became quickly transformed into a group of wicked, beaked demons, who urged the man to grasp the sword and brandish it aloft. He did so, with an unexplained reluctance, and cut the air above with quick strokes. He felt power, brutal and bold, coarse and disturbing, vicious and awesome. The demons' black eyes gleamed, and lightning bolts lit the sky.

He lay down the weapon and strode purposefully towards the multicolored shoes. He was magically and intently drawn to the first door, and as the horrid demons tried to stop him with shrill shrieks and clawed attacks, he merely brushed them aside.

He approached the door, stooped down and touched the shoes. The feel was smooth and the colors were pleasing to the eye. He put them on his feet, laced them to the hilt and stood tall before the first door.

Instantly, darkness became light and bright sunshine filled the heavens. With the shoes upon his feet, the man they called Quarterback experienced a glowing energy and supreme contentment unlike anything he had ever felt.

Beams of goodness pulsed through his muscles and concepts of truth, fairness and justice flashed across his brow. All power was his, but this time it felt right.

The first door lay before him. There was no doubt now; this place was for him, the only choice. But as he grasped the handle, he became seized with the knowledge that the destiny he was about to fulfill was not his alone.

Quarterback turned the knob, thrust forward the door and bolted upright in bed. It was 6AM, and sweet Sally lay softly to his left. The sun streamed through the venetian blinds and the world never looked brighter. His eyes scanned the bedroom and fell to rest on the pigskin, ever present in his life. The months of gruel, the years of waiting, the vivid dream, his renewed feelings of purpose and power—all could mean only one thing. This was . . .

THE YEAR!

Remember that well known song "The Ballad of the Green Berets?" Put these words to that tune, and the result is . . .

The Ballad of the Blue Wall

Fighting Giants from all sides,
Fierce Blue Wall, that never dies;
Fleet foot backs, that rush with pride,
Quarterbacks, that lead our side.

Goal line stand, by men of steel,
Tackling linebackers, who sack with zeal;
Cornerbacks, who grab and steal,
Ends who have, QB's for meals.

Golden toes boot winning goals,
That sail right through, those yellow poles;
Tenacious "D", that plugs the holes,
Those winning men, of heart and soul.

Red and Blue, spells Eagle's doom,
Cowboys' losses, and Redskins' gloom;
On any day, our greatness looms,
Giants and victory, they're bride and groom!

Famous Farrenkopf of Fishkill

According to Dee Nixon of Fishkill, New York, die-hard Giants fan Charlie Farrenkopf has converted the entire village (near Poughkeepsie) into Big Blue rooters.

She writes: "During the day he is a quiet, conservative IBM executive, but during football season, he becomes a totally whacko Giants fan!"

On Saturday afternoons before Giants games, he parades down Main Street, stopping traffic while walking his two big 200 pound Newfoundland dogs, each wearing their custom made Giants jerseys. He himself tips his famous orange Giants hat, and reminds everyone to watch the game on TV.

His lucky team hat never seems to come off his head. "We had to beg him to remove the hat long enough to look presentable for his marriage ceremony to Anne Marie, a lovely girl from Norway."

Charlie erected a 20-foot flagpole in Dee's front yard, and every Sunday the Giants play, he hoises a huge hand lettered blue and white flag he made. The flag's height is directly proportional to how the Giants are doing that day!

Charlie's first anniversary dinner was a romantic one . . . he and Ann . . . and Dave Jennings and the entire Chamber of Commerce! "In the fall, his apartment becomes a Giants museum to house his treasures."

I can picture the look on Dee's face as she concludes her letter: "Who am I to question the taste of such a dedicated Giants fan!? There is no stopping him."

Beware of Flying Objects

Giants fans take losing to heart, without question. Family and friends of John Cook of Sedus, New York, steer clear of him when the Giants have dropped one.

Because of his died-in-the-wool antics for over 30 years, John has developed the reputation of venting his frustrations upon whichever objects happen to be close at hand.

After Giants victories, his home is neat, tidy and clean. But should the Giants lose, especially a heartbreaker, the place looks like a tornado came through it.

There is one person who loves John's behavior, and loves it when he gets this way: the owner of the local hardware store. Break a bottle, John!

Long Term Planning

This is an almost completely unedited letter from Ken Zelenakas of Colonia, NJ. Note the colorful description Ken chooses when writing about following the Giants throughout the year.

"Being a Giants fan is a way of life. True loyalists, are in every sense of the word, zealots. A day rarely passes without my thoughts focused on the Giant organization, and with each new season, my obsession grows a little bit more."

"The low point of the year is when the season ends, because it's at this time when the new season is farthest away. During this lag period, I spend a great deal of time evaluating the needs of the Giants and anticipating the upcoming NFL draft. Throughout the entire year, I'm constantly scanning the newspapers just to read any article that may be about or related to the Giants."

"Even though I live in Central Jersey, I plan several trips with my friends to training camp, just to be among the electricity and excitement they generate. For me this is a time of exhilaration. I'm swamped with a deluge of great hope, for the beginning of each season conveys for me a new dawn; this season will be the one!"

"Opening day, like training camp, is a special one. I start this day with a definite plan in mind—to observe, with the skill of a great scientist, and to record in my memory each detail of the day—everything from what I wear, what I eat and so forth. This is important because, if the Giants win, this process must be repeated the following week without deviation."

"A loss throws me full speed into a state of depression which is so bad, I'm unable to deal with it in a reasonable manner. I feel as if it's my own fault, because I ate the wrong food or put on the wrong color socks. A mixed state of depression and irrationality is upon me. By Wednesday, I'm looking forward to the next game, with renewed enthusiasm as I will never lose hope."

"My weekends, vacations, everything . . . is planned around the Giants. I'm not sure what the magnetism is about, but whatever it is, it has overtaken me and I love them! I've requested that when I die, I want to be cremated and have my ashes spread on the 50 yard line at Giants stadium."

Ken, I'm sure the rest of the millions of Giants fans share the exact sentiments you put into words!

The Llabtoof Gang

Back in 1965, Dave Burke organized the LLABTOOF Club, a group of die-hards which travels to an away game every year. The group has doubled since their inception, and has a center of operations in a restaurant/bar in Beacon, New York called Mi-Ro.

They leave on Thursdays and return Monday night, and since 1966 they've been to almost every NFL city. Aged 18 to 72, this group went to Atlanta in 1981, Los Angeles in '82, and will journey out to Kansas City this season. They're repeating K.C. this year because the first away game that the Giants won was against the Chiefs back in 1974. Let's hope history repeats itself!

Oh, by the way . . . in case you haven't figured it out yet, LLABTOOF is the word "football" spelled backwards.

Philosophy 101

Mitch Bator of Edison, New Jersey, has his own philosophy on being a Giants fan: "If you're not totally into the Giants, you're not really experiencing life!"

To support his beliefs, Mitch has everything in his life revolve around the Giants. His room is painted Giants blue, as is his Volkswagen, which has numerous Giants bumperstickers. Of course, his license plates say NYG.

His collectibles are numerous, including Giants pennants, books, glasses, mugs, ashtray, and so forth. So is his wardrobe—Giants pants, shirts, scarves, ties, etc.

Mitch hits all the games, many away contests, plus the Giants basketball games, fund raisers, training camp and more.

After reading about other die-hards, this behavior may not seem too extreme. But it gets better. He gets all the Giants publications, tunes into and participates on the Giants' coaches radio shows, and maintains a VCR library of Giants victories.

Here's the kicker: Mitch will not get married between July (training camp) and February, and April is also not available (draft month). Mitch's first son will be named Lawrence T. People think Mitch is going through a phase . . . but we all know better, don't we?

United We Stand . . .

Al Barrett has the kind of job most of us would envy— he's a high fashion and commercial photographer, enjoying an artistic line of work, rubbing elbows with the famous and in general, enjoying his craft. You wouldn't think that behind his studio doors would lurk a die-hard Giants fan, who looks more forward more to getting out for a Giants club luncheon than he does to developing a print of a famous model.

Well, Al Barrett is just that person. WCBS interviewed Al twice, following him around on two Giant Sundays. What emerged from the tape he sent me was an interesting recollection of the 1960's, a time at which Al basked in the glory of a Giants championship team.

He remembers The Section Five Club (now the Kickoff Club, see Chapter 10) at The Polo Grounds. His biggest thrill was having dinner with Giant greats Y.A. Tittle and Del Shofner. Another was meeting Allie Sherman in the locker room. Former star Darrell Dess is the Godfather for Barrett's youngest son.

Like Al, I too, feel fortunate, having been able to start and maintain my own business, write and publish several books, and have a nice home and family. But whether you work nine to five or own the company, there is a bond between Giants fans that ignores what you do for a living or how much money you earn. That, in my opinion, is the most unique aspect of Giants fans. We are the world's largest fraternity, treating strangers like brothers in our singleminded pursuit of the Super Bowl ring.

That is the real purpose to this story. When people say "we're all in the same boat" it couldn't be more true. We are—young or old, rich or poor, educated or not—all in this thing together, and I, and I'm sure Al would agree, have never seen anything unite people more than the Giants.

Dan Timoney . . . A license to be a Giants fan!

Our Fans Are Unreal!

Ed Croke is the Director Of Media Services for the Giants, and amongst the preparation of all kinds of goodies for the press, he also edits the newsletter which Giant season ticket holders receive.

Consequently, Ed gets stacks of mail from fans, both around the country and around the world. I met with Ed last March and he recalled his favorite stories and fans.

Not only does Ed get mail from fans, but a lot of memorabilia as well. Adorning his wall is a red, white and blue needlepoint of the Giants helmet, donated by a Giants fan. Among the knick knacks found in his office is a crystal ball and ceramic tray, both with miniature Giant helmets, footballs and other things. A homemade bumper sticker, mugs, cups and other items submitted by fans gives Ed's office the appearance of a Giants general store.

Ed's mail is postmarked from places like Salem, NH; San Diego, CA and Egypt . . . not Egypt, New York but Egypt, the place with the pyramids.

Two of the Giant crazies, "Crazy Louie" and "Crazy Charlie", regularly write Ed. Charlie travels the world and regularly sends the Giant staff postcards from exotic places. They all read the same: "Ed, there's a 6'5 prospect out here in the pyramids . . . I think you should invite him to summer camp." Charlie flies into training camp, flies to games and is considered by some to be the Giants overseas scout!

Crazy Charlie isn't the only fan who finds great future ballplayers for the team. Dozens of fans have 8 foot, 400 pound monsters who can do the hundred in 3.3 waiting in the wings.

During our meeting, Ed went through many years of newsletters, recalling with nostalgic surprise the crazy things fans have written him about over the years. "Take Archie of Salem, New Hampshire. He attends training camp (doesn't everyone) and comes to every game. He tapes all the games, and watches them during the off season. In addition to subscribing to the Giants Newsweekly, he gets three New York papers delivered regularly so he can follow the team."

Ed recalls Martin Wall, a long time ticket holder, who had never missed a game until he went into the Navy. Sent overseas, he applied for emergency leave to attend home games. Unfortunately "the Navy had no sense of humor." Marty's streak continued after his service.

And there's Marie Niedermeier of Fairfield, Connecticut, who, with her 12 children; see every game. Harry B. Howe, of the U.S. Virgin Islands, flies in for home game weekends. Emma Hansen of Leonia, New Jersey has been a season ticket holder for 55 years, and who continues to attend games . . . being well over 80 years old!

Running neck-in-neck with Emma is Mike Winston of Lakehurst, who recalls paying 50 cents for general admission seats in the Polo Grounds in 1925. He's been with the Giants in Yankee Stadium, Yale Bowl and now the Meadowlands.

"We have many groups who charter planes to go to away games. We help with the arrangements. There's a group in Poughkeepsie, New York, called LLABTOOF, that's football spelled backwards. They put money into a pot during the year and then pick an away game, and their whole group, with over 100 members, travels to the game. So many people came out to San Francisco for the playoff game a few years back that we took the entire hotel!"

Ed recalls the story of the fire in a Rhode Island bar in 1979. A fireman rushed into the inferno to save the bar's most valuable possession . . . not the cash register, but a framed, signed photo of Giants superstar Sam Huff, with the owner.

Perhaps one of Ed's fondest memories is the story involving actor Elliott Gould, who is a die-hard Giants fan.

"Before Elliott became well known, he played summer stock theaters up in New England. He would listen to the games on a transistor radio when he played Sunday matinees. Waiting in the wings, he'd be huddled over the radio, intent on not missing a single play. Often he would miss his cue cards, and sometimes blow his lines. After his bit on the stage, he'd run back to the side, get the radio and continue listening!"

Up, Up and Away!

Ron and Cathy Haldas of Selden, New York, have a 6 foot plastic balloon replica of a Giant's player. Filled with helium, it perches atop their roof during special games. It hung on

78

the billboards during those years at Yale Bowl. It's been t
the new stadium, only to be denied admission.

But the Haldas' haven't given up . . . their balloon is in
storage . . . ready and waiting for the day they can bring
to the SuperBowl. A job well done . . . and when we get t
the SuperBowl, there'll be plenty of people to help smugg
it in, you can bet!

I Get This Feeling . . .

Gary Marzolla is a thinking man's Giants fan. Ever since
he was a kid, he not only roots for the Giants, but seems
have an uncanny ability to predict what's going to happer
2–5 minutes before it does.

Gary claims to have predicted the squibb kick mishap
against Washington, the last minute loss to St. Louis and
numerous other outcomes where everyone else watching
game was sure the game was won.

His explanation for this ability lies in what he does. For
years now, Gary has been deeply thinking and mulling o

every Giant play. By now, he feels he knows the psychology of the way the team plays, and can use this accumulated knowledge to help the team. He is currently engaged in a campaign to get his voice heard by the coaching staff.

What's more amazing about Gary's obsession is that it gets him sick. No, not a throbbing headache or upset stomach like the rest of us, but back pains, migraines that last for weeks and other undiagnosed illnesses that keep him out of work, and as a kid, out of school. Doctors couldn't explain his fevers nor cure his sudden attacks. A Giants victory, of course, could, and did!

It all started, according to Gary, during the 1958 season (Gary was 9 years old). "I can remember a game where the Giants had to beat the Browns to force a playoff. It was snowing like hell that day. The score was 10–10, and there had to be 6 inches of snow on the ground . . . no one could see the yard markers. And Summerall comes in and kicks this field goal. And we couldn't even see the players . . . that's how hard it was snowing. The ball was in the air, and we couldn't see the ball going through the uprights. We beat 'em 13–10, which got us into the playoffs."

"Next week, we had to win again, which we did. And then we got into the playoffs and lost a heartbreaker to the Colts. Those two victories and the one nightmarish loss left me devastated."

I asked Gary if he could remember any event in his life, outside of the sports area, that had such an impact as the trio of games in that '58 season. His answer, after much thought, was no!

Gary recalls this experience as the single event which started his Giants fanaticism, one which has reached the innermost corners of his mind, and one which he takes to heart. Because of his intense concentration and thinking about Giant playcalling and the psychology of football, Gary would love nothing better than to assist the coaches on the sidelines.

Attention Giants . . . anyone want to give this guy a tryout?

And They're Off . . .

It seems as if everyone is naming things after Giants players. The bullies in school call themselves the 'Crunch Bunch' and every kid that plays defense calls himself 'LT'.

But there's a horse, who as of April of this year, was eyeing the Kentucky Derby. This horse, named after for a famous Giants quarterback, led every step of the way to win at Aqueduct. The horse's name . . . Chas Conerly, of course!

By The Numbers!

Wearing Giants jerseys is not enough for Charles T. Stelzer Jr. and his buddies. He and his friends have complete home and away uniforms, which they wear for all the games, corresponding, of course, to where the game is played.

He says "My number is 10, of course, for Brad Van Pelt. In the past I have had number 64 for John Mendenhall and number 38 for Bob Tucker. As players are traded, we retire their numbers. Our creed is never to have an out of date jersey."

When Charlie and his friends watch the games, one only has to wonder if they call each other by name . . . or by the

David Helmstetter, Paul Stevens and Charles Stelzer Jr. check out their uniforms for the '83 season.

Behind Every Great Giants Fan . . .

I'm amazed at the number of letters we get from people about to be married during a Giants game. Maybe there should be a law against marriages on Sunday afternoons during football season.

For the most part, however, we're very lucky, as our wives seem to care about us enough to overlook this major flaw we all have. Witness this incident from Ralph Vaiatica of Parsippany, New Jersey.

"On Oct. 21st, 1951, the Giants were playing the Eagles at the Polo Grounds. I was listening to the game on radio, and at half-time, I had to go out for an important engagement—I was getting married."

He continues, "At the end of the ceremony, in the vestibule of the church, while accepting congratulations from friends and relatives, my eyes caught those of my buddies. All I could think about was how the Giants did."

"To this day, my wife Fanny of 32 years has often teased me about that day, asking 'Was that the only thing on your mind at the time?'"

She's taken it well, and on this couple's first anniversary (paper), she bought him a book, "The New York Giants" which he treasures to this day. We just wonder if he remembers the date because of his wedding, or because of a victory over the Eagles!

A Good Day For Summerall

Giants fans take a lot of ribbing, kidding and downright nastiness from fans of opposing teams. Especially in the stretch of losing seasons.

Michael Lesco of Levittown, New York, recalls a 33–0 Giant victory this way: "Many years ago the Giants went five or six games without scoring a touchdown, but they still won a game or two on field goals. Finally they won a game, by a big count, 33–0. Looking at the back page headline announcing this terrific score, one anti-Giants fan said 'That darned Summerall kicked eleven field goals!'"

Good Luck Giants!

When the Giants made it to the playoffs against San Francisco two years ago, the Monday before the game I got a call from one of my retail advertising accounts, Walter Bauman Jewelers. He gave me the copy for that week's ad for The Star Ledger, and asked that at the top of the ad, in big bold letters, we write "Good luck to the Giants in San Francisco!" Unfortunately, that by itself wasn't enough. If only he had run a full page ad that week!

Sold on the Giants!

How does one first become a Giants fan? Few of us can answer that question, but Robert Lopa of Northvale, New Jersey, can, and it's an interesting answer.

"I became a Giants fan in a very strange way. Until 1978 I had never watched a football game (Ed: highly questionable statement, but I'll let it go) but when I was in the hospital recuperating from a heart attack, I got my first taste of football . . . and the Giants. While I was in bed and unable to get up, a nurse asked me if I wanted to watch TV. I said 'fine' and she turned on the set, and there was a football game—the Giants. At that moment she was called away and couldn't change the channel as I wanted her to. Since I had an IV, I couldn't either. I had to watch the game because the nurse didn't return til much later. By the end of the game, I became a Giants fan!"

As we all know, it doesn't matter how, but only that you are a true-blue Giants fan.

Hedge Your Bets

One fan writes us about something we all can relate to: betting on the Giants. Because of the agonizing way in which games are won or lost by our team, betting has left more people frustrated than the outcomes of the games themselves.

Bill Freda of Valley Stream, New York, writes "Regardless of what Pete Rozelle says, most self-respecting football fans have money on NFL games each week. A friend of mine, a fellow Giants fan, once gave me some profitable advice that has spared me much suffering over the years. I call it Gary's Golden Rule, and it has two parts:

(1) Never bet on the Giants.
(2) Never bet against the Giants."

Bill and Gary, now that sounds like something we'd hear in Philosophy 101. But it is true, against the spread the Giants do very, very well. But for pure win/loss, it's more risky.

Say a Little Prayer . . .

It seems as if back in the days of Yankee Stadium, many of the players stayed in a local hotel, and on Sundays, many went to a church nearby for the 9AM mass.

A man who worked at the Church during those golden years reports seeing many Giants faces, but the highlight of the service was the closing prayer. The pastor always requested the congregation say a special prayer: "For God, country and a Giant victory!"

The last year the Pastor led the congregation in that prayer was the year the Giants went on to win the championship. Hint, hint guys!

Sweet Dreams

Ask any Giants fan what they dream about and the answer is the same: SuperBowl victory. Like another fan portrayed in this book, James DiGesu of North Arlington, NJ has dreams the Giants management might be wise to listen to.

Jim writes, "Back in 1976, about three months before the signing of Larry Csonka, I dreamt he had signed. When I told my family about this, they wrote it off as a 16 year old with a very active sub-conscious. They apologized when it became official."

That's OK, but Jim's next dream, during the '81 season, could have made a lot of people rich! "The Giants had been on the playoff hunt, and they were 8–5 going into the finale with Dallas. The Tuesday before, I awoke and remembered the dream I had the night before, about the Giants battling the mighty cowboys."

"I dreamt Joe Danelo tied the game, forced an overtime and won it with a field goal. That's what happened, and propelled the Giants into the playoffs for the first time in 18 years. When I told people about this dream, I told them to bet the ranch on the Giants; they were still skeptical. Their loss, not mine."

Well Jim, let's just you and me keep this a secret. Call me with your next dream, and I won't tell a soul. Then only you and I can laugh on the way to the bank!

True Loves . . .

Henry DeBianchi, the founder of The Football Giants Fan Club, now has two loves in his life! You know the first, and the other is his new wife Nancy. Henry proposed on December 19, 1981 . . . ring a bell.

That was the day the Giants defeated Dallas in dramatic overtime fashion, 13–10 at Giants stadium. Henry remembers it well: "I vividly recall that day, and always will. I had the engagement ring in my jacket pocket all game long. Each time an exciting play was made by our Giants I'd jump up and down, and check my pocket to make sure the ring didn't pop out. When Joe Danelo hit that 35-yard field goal to win the game, Nancy and I jumped up and down, hugging each other as tears filled our eyes."

After the victory, we headed for a dinner celebration at the Giants Stadium Club restaurant. After dinner I asked Nancy to marry me . . . over dessert. It was a double celebration at Table #19 on the 19th of December."

Having received so many letters from husbands of football widows, it was great to get this one. Perhaps this football romance should be distributed as required reading to every Giants fan household . . .

CHAPTER 7

The ultimate
Giants fan!

The Ultimate Giants Fan

Almost every letter I received on this project was from someone who claimed he was the #1 fan, or from a spouse that was sure her husband was the best, most loyal Giants fan around.

As you can probably guess, choosing our ultimate Giants fan for 1983 was no easy task, and I suspect it will get harder for next year's edition of "Those Crazy Giants Fans".

But, after much analysis, the verdict is in: my choice for The Ultimate Giants fan, and family, is Ed Sulem, his wife Betsy, their son and daughter, of Gloversville, New York.

Driving through the sleepy town of Gloversville (four, yes four hours from the Meadowlands), which features your basic suburban environment, middle class homes, families with two kids and a dog, you get a sense that this is a normal town, with normal people living in it.

The first clue you get that a crazed Giant fan lives among the residents is the mailbox at the end of Ed Sulem's driveway. It's got a Giants pennant stuck in it which lets every passer-by know what team Ed likes. But that, you say, may not be so out of the ordinary. But, I say, that's just the beginning.

Pulling into the driveway, you spot the next piece of incriminating evidence: twin personalized license plates. Betsy's Volkswagen bug has NYGFW-1 and the family wagon has NYGF-1. We'll leave it to you to guess what the letters stand for.

The picture above is typical of the Sulem family: dad in basic coaching gear, complete with headphones, mom in mourning as a football widow (clue to W in her license plate), son Bobby as football player to be, daughter Nancy in complete cheerleading outfit, and dog Martha (guess why that name) sitting outside red, white and blue doghouse on Giants mat. An American flag is added for effect . . . now that's a Giant family! Good friends of the Sulems refer to their house as "Giants Stadium North!"

Let's begin our visit with the Sulems with the smallest living members of the family, and work our way up to Big Ed, sometimes known as "Tuna" to friends, family and Giants players, coaches and management.

Walking to the back of the house, we see a miniature set of yellow goal posts, with a red, white and blue birdhouse sitting between the uprights. By now you simply must have guessed the Giants' colors. Note the little bird house mounted on the tree . . . that's for rookies! We understand that Ed only allows blue jays, robin red breasts or white doves to gain entrance to the birdhouse. Other birds such as cardinals and eagles, and animals such as bears and rams are not allowed on the premises. We can see why!

Next on the evolutionary ladder is their dog Martha, who lives in a comfortable dog house. The colors you already know. It must be easy decorating a house in only three colors!

Anyhow, Martha, the dog, can't complain. She's got her house, her water bowl, a Giants bumper sticker and a flag. Everyone knows she was named after the woman who sings the national anthem at Giants Stadium. I also have it from good sources that Martha has been known to "hold it in until the Giants win!" You think we suffer during losing seasons; think of Martha next time we're on the short end of the score.

The inside of the Sulem residence is pretty much normal, until, that is, you come upon Ed's son Bobby's room. Everything here says Giants: penants, pictures, posters, football cards, and more. If we held a contest for the largest collection of Giants memorabilia in a kid's room, Bobby would walk away with the title

Anyhow, Bobby can never forget whose team he roots for; he's reminded every time he walks into his room. His future includes being a Giant as well. All of this Giant fever at such a young age has been brought about by his dad, who has arranged for many of the Giant players to pose with Bobby. His wall features signed photos by the biggest, the best and the friendliest of the Giants. In fact, Bobby probably knows more about each Giant (by the numbers, of course) than the respective Giant knows about himself! Bobby's memory includes such items as number, name, position, college played for, rookie year, and much more. He knows the coaches in their order of service. Gads, we sometimes wonder if Bobby has room in his memory for things like algebra and American history. Actually, his folks tell us Bobby does well in school.

Bobby with Jeter, Simms and Carson.

Ed's parents are totally oblivious to the Giant mania in the Sulem household. When they first saw Bobby's red, white and blue enclave, Ed's mom thought it was so patriotic. Some things are better left unchallenged!

Bobby wouldn't be such a big fan if not for the encouragement he gets from dad, the understanding from mom, or the support from his sister, who, at this stage in her life, is content cheerleading for her brother to be a Giant one day. She doesn't understand how Bobby and Ed can travel to a Giants practice and stay there all day without getting bored!

When important things happen to the Giants or to Ed, people in their lives respond. Upon his promotion, one of the bank employees baked a football cake, featuring helmets for the Giants and Dallas, their foe that week. You can guess which helmet was devoured to the battle cry of "let's eat our opponents for dessert!"

Happy Holidays

Will The Real Ray Perkins PLEASE STAND UP !

Happy Holidays

W O W !
47 GIANT "Supporters"
All In One Room !

Peace on Earth

I HAVE A LICENSE
WHAT'S YOUR EXCUSE?

Peace on Earth

MR. SULEM, CAN I
HAVE YOUR AUTOGRAPH?

Peace on earth

THE GIANT HAS LANDED
1979 IS OUR YEAR

For those people who never get to Ed Sulem's place, there are his Christmas cards . . . the ones he gets (from Wellington Mara) and the ones he sends to 75 fans around the country . . . personalized cards with pictures of Ed's involvement with the Giants.

So that's it for the Sulem home. Nice, American, and full of red, white and blue. But this is only where Ed Sulem's love affair with the Giants begins.

Since Ed likes to attend practice sessions over five hours away at Pace University and never misses a home game (a mere four hours drive), he has a problem: time. That's probably why he became a banker, so he can take advantage of banker's hours to meet all his commitments to his team.

If you thought, as I did, that his office at the bank would be devoid of Giant artifacts, we underestimated Ed. He has autographed pictures of George Young, Ray Perkins and Bill Parcells, hanging where prospective loan applicants can't help noticing. But that wouldn't be so bad if that was it. But no. Throughout the bank, nobody calls him Ed. No one addresses him as Mr. Sulem. To everyone at his financial institution, he's "coach".

So Ed has managed to blend a somewhat normal life as a banker with Giant practices, games and obsessions. Getting back to training camp . . .

Ed is as a familiar face at Giants training camp as Lawrence Taylor, Phil Simms, Brad Van Pelt or Dave Jennings. In fact, Ed has originated many of the loveable nicknames borne by Giants stars, among them "The Toe," "The Nose" and "Floyd the Flame." You guess who.

The coaches are not exempt from Ed's presence, and Monday morning quarterbacking. Sometimes the players have confused him with former head coach Ray Perkins.

Ed's conferences with Perkins about the game and the team are a part of training camp. His presence on the sidelines during a game prove time and time again to the players that Giants fans are indeed devoted.

Ed's wife Betsy knows where to find Ed if she needs him. Forget about calling the bank. Forget about calling the local candy store or diner. Ed can be reached at Giants training camp, but he usually doesn't like to be disturbed when he's working.

Getting to the game is another story. Ed hasn't missed a home game in years, despite the fact that he doesn't own season tickets. He still drives four hours to the games, knowing he'll luck out by getting tickets from friends, or find scalpers who have gotten rich off him.

When Ed doesn't go to the game alone, he travels with a contingent from the area, who always stop at the same diner in Kingston, who eat the same exact meal they did last time if the Giants won, and who park in the same place at the stadium parking lot (9C). The group at 9C includes fans from New York, New Jersey and Connecticut. During the off season, they all correspond by mail.

Ed will do anything to see an away game. In 1978, after learning the local station would not be carrying a certain away Game, Ed called the station and tried to convince them to show the game. He even wrote a letter to the FCC questioning the station's right to show a different game. When the station wouldn't give in, Ed rented a small plane, at a cost of $120, hired a pilot, and flew to Long Island, where Ed's sister-in-law lives. Without warning, they landed, jumped the fence to her home (she lives near the airport), watched the game, ate dinner, and flew home! The Giants beat Kansas City that day, and the trip, according to Ed, "was well worth it!"

For one December home game, Ed organized a trip with 7–8 other fans in a travel trailer. It was near Christmastime, and Ed decorated a tree with red, white and blue satin balls (new religious dogma). His slogan for the day was "I'm dreaming of a winning season!" Not only that, Betsy told me Ed sometimes has dreams about the games.

Once Ed had tickets to a game, and sat right in front of one of the glass enclosed suites, in which there was a TV. After each play, he was able to turn around and catch the instant replay. When the people in the booth blocked the TV from him, he yelled at them to move over . . . which they did!

In 1982, Ed flew to Miami to see a Giants exhibition game which was nationally televised. In order to get a sideline pass, he worked delivering ice to the lockerroom. Betsy taped the entire game, just to have Ed preserved forever, on the sidelines with the players and coaches during the game!

Going to the games and viewing them in any way he can isn't all Ed does. Every year he throws pre-draft, pre-playoff and pre-super bowl parties for his so-called upstate coaching staff.

While banker's hours make much of this possible, Ed does take off one day every year. His birthday? No. Guess.

Draft day, silly! Yes, he monitors the Giants progress in the annual draft of college players. He has a house party for the event, at which attendance increases every year! Before his draft parties, Ed once drove to New York the night before the draft, and was at the hotel at 7AM just to get in line to see the Giants' first round pick! Holy mackerel!!!

When Ed's home watching the game on Sunday afternoons, there is certain protocol that the family follows. No plans are ever made on game days. No one is invited over to watch the game except for selected Giant fans. Total silence is required, and dinner is planned around the completion of the game.

Ed will not accept any phone calls during the game, as he cannot miss a play. With Bobby and Nancy, he carries on during the game, usually very loudly. Betsy can tell by the type and decibel level of the sounds coming from the living room how the Giants are doing. If the Giants lose, the family can expect silence from Ed for the rest of that night, and sometimes into the following week, depending on the severity of the loss. After the fateful Philadelphia game, he sat completely still for three hours. According to Betsy, "he didn't move or talk. I wasn't even sure if he was breathing!"

When the Giants win, Ed wears a blue shirt with his Giants tie into work the next day. Everyone at work knows by his Monday morning dress who won the day before.

I wanted very much to travel and talk to Ed and Betsy up in Gloversville but time wouldn't permit. So Ed sat the family down and recorded an hour cassette tape which they sent down to me. About Ed's obsession with the Giants, Betsy says, "Ed was never a real big Giants fan when we got married 14 years ago. I think his obsession developed over the years, probably as a result of my family. Ed is very strong willed, and coming into a family of anti-Giants fan people, the more they spoke out against the Giants, the more Ed defended them and loved them. I'd never ask him to choose between me and the Giants, because I think I'd come out #2 in the end."

On his dedication, she says, "Ed lives the role of Giants fan all year long. I don't think there's a day where the colors red, white and blue aren't related to the Giants. Even our Christmas presents have something to do with the Giants. In any season or at any occasion throughout the year, he's a total fan."

Ed's dedication to the Giants has given him more than a team to root for on Sunday afternoons. It's brought him friendships for himself and his wife; and a thrill for his kids that not many kids can get. But most of all, its been a second life, a remove-the-pinstripe-suit-change-into-football gear fantasy most of us just dream of.

In fact, when Betsy first wrote us about her husband, her description included the following:

> Before I continue my explanation, I should point out that he is a somewhat sane person who is a reasonably successful bank manager, living a normal average middle class life; except for his NEW YORK GIANT OBSESSIONS.

This, directly from the person who lives with him, who is sent red, white and blue flowers on her birthday and Valentine's Day, confirms our belief that the basis for Ed's fanaticism lies in his healthy desire to be more than a spectator . . . more than a TV watcher. It's a dream he's chosen to act on.

C'mon . . . how many times have you wished you could be on the field, hugging Danelo after he's just kicked a game-winning field goal? I think that's a part of all of us . . . and Giant fan extraordinaire Ed Sulem has made that dream come true.

Betsy's letter to us closes with a sentiment she feels out of pride for her husband. I suspect many other wives would say the same for other reasons, like health, marital stability or widowhood. She writes:

> For his sake, your sake, and all other loyal Giant fans, I hope that this year will truly be THE YEAR.

Hats off to the Sulem family, four hours away, in Gloversville, New York.

CHAPTER 8

Beyond being a Giants fan

Heartwarming

We've seen, so far, that Giants fans are extraordinary. That they go to any length to see, listen or get to the stadium to watch the game. That they devour every play and take every win or loss personally.

In the course of researching this book, I came across another Giants fan who goes beyond being a fan. Sure, this person, with his wife and two sons, wouldn't miss a Giants game. They've got Giants memorabilia, including lucite embedded tickets to the first Meadowlands game, coming out of their ears. Their young son defends the Giants better than any cornerback, lawyer or bouncer. He has written a book report for school on a Giants book, and has drawn pictures in his art class (it looks great in color)—see next page.

This is another true Giants family, with mom, dad and two boys thoroughly caught up with the team.

But Charles "Corky" Raab goes beyond being a Giants fan. Corky, as everyone knows him, demonstrated to me, and to hundreds of other people over the years, that what he does puts him on another level, one which solidifies the family feeling felt between fans, players, management and presidents of major corporations.

Corky operates a Budweiser distributorship in Nyack, New York, about a half-hour north of the stadium. Through people he knew, Corky heard that handicapped kids from hospitals around the metropolitan area would be coming to Giant home games. Upon hearing this, Corky called his friend George Cool, a caterer from Haverstraw, and they met at the first home game, in October of 1976.

George brought the food in a mobile home and Corky brought beer and soft drinks in his brightly decorated van . . . dubbed the Bud Van.

"We got there about two hours before the game," Corky recalls, "and the handicapped kids ate and drank and partied. They then went in to watch the game, and when they came out, we fed them dinner and gave them more to drink. You should have seen them."

On the way down to the next home game, Corky spoke to George on the CB, who said "Corky, we have a surprise for you". Upon reaching the stadium parking area, the Meadowlands security directed us to the first parking space in the handicapped zone. Thus began Corky's relationship with the people at the Meadowlands, who took their hats off to this person in a van who would donate beer and drink to handicapped kids at every single Giant home game. That spot along the curb became known as "Corky's" spot.

Today, Corky's van is accompanied by a newly converted school bus, painted red, white and blue, with comfortable seats inside. The van and the bus make a welcome sight to the 30–40 handicapped kids who come to every game.

Before and after the game there are always about 125 people near the van and bus, including the kids, friends, and after the game, players. The Giants players make time after each game to be with the kids, not just to say hello in passing, but to spend some real, meaningful time with them.

The scene, as I've come to know it, inspires only one word of description: heartwarming. For it is something very special that Corky, George, the security people and the players do for these kids.

Corky tells the story of little Eddie O'Grady, whose dad was shot and killed in the Brink's robbery several years back. "We had dinner one day with the family, and the little boy, still very much depressed, mentioned that he loved the Giants and hated Dallas." It just so happened that the Giants/Dallas game was coming up shortly, so Corky said "Eddie, you're going to the Giants/Dallas game. "So I called up Dave Jennings and said 'Dave, I have little Eddie O'Grady with me, and I need three tickets for the Giants/Dallas game.' I explained to Dave the situation with Eddie's dad. Dave said 'No problem, Corky'."

"The day of the game, Dave sent a messenger who came to the van and asked me my name. When I said 'Corky', she handed me three tickets, compliments of Dave Jennings." So Eddie, with no dad but a bunch of second fathers already beginning to form, saw the Giants beat Dallas.

But that wasn't all of this story. When Eddie arrived at the stadium, Corky talked to the state police. They knew about Eddie's dad, who, of course, was a policeman. "When we got there, one of the troopers put Eddie into a car, gave him a tour of the stadium, and then drove him out onto the field, so he could walk around while the Giants were practicing. Eddie was then taken to the press booth, and after the game, all the players came out and signed Eddie's program. They all spent time with Eddie, had pictures taken. It was a great experience!"

Corky has gotten close to Jennings and many of the Giant players, as well as coaches, management, and many of the corporate presidents who attend the games. There will be times when Corky will take one of the kids up to the WNEW radio booth, and he, along with Jack Thayer of the station, his wife, and other important people, will join forces to make this kid have the day of his life. It's something none of these people have to do, but they do it anyway, and it works.

Corky enjoys the story of his first meeting with Jennings, who was to become a close friend and contribute constantly to Corky's efforts. "One time at the stadium, my friend George called me over and said 'Corky, I want you to meet my friend Dave Jennings'. I said 'Dave, how are you, nice to meet you. Where do you come from, and what do you do for a living?' And Dave says 'I'm from New York now, and I'm the punter for the Giants!' I'll never live that down. Still to this day, I'm harassed about it."

The bond between Corky, George and the handicapped kids has grown. "Whenever we need a ticket, we've got offers from all the kids. Once I offered to pay one of the handicapped kids for a ticket. Boy was that a mistake." The young man gave Corky the tickets, and said "After what you've done for us, no way. Don't insult me!"

Corky is a man who enjoys life to the fullest, and enjoys helping people who aren't as fortunate as he. The look on the handicapped kids' faces "is all I need to keep me going".

One of Corky's favorite stories is about the son of a friend, who had 9 kids, but only one boy. When he was 16, this boy dove into a swimming pool and something went wrong. The boy was paralyzed from the neck down, with movement only in his hands. His family spent over thirty thousand dollars to renovate the house.

"We decided to have a fund raising event to help this family out" according to Corky. "It was a joint effort between the Rockland County Liquor Dealers Association, Corky and his dad's firm, Raso Beer Distributors, the policemen, and many friends and family. We had a dinner for the boy, and over 1500 people came."The boy is a Giants fan, and his favorite player is Dave Jennings. Once again I called on Dave, who came through. Very few people knew Dave was coming to the dinner, least of all the boy in the wheelchair. When Dave came over and was introduced, the look on this kid's face was just unbelievable! He couldn't believe his favorite player was right next to him. Dave spent 20 minutes, and promised to send him some Giants clothing. Less than a week later, the clothing arrived. That night, we raised $38,000 dollars for the family."

So that's the side of Corky that inspired the title of this chapter. It's this type of "going beyond the call of duty" that is so rare, but when it happens, it's beautiful.

As we continue to salute the dedication of Giants fans, our hats go off to Corky and his Bud Van, George and his catering bus, the Meadowlands security, the police, the players, and everyone who shows there's more to being a Giants fan than rooting for the team.

Corky's two boys, future heartwarmers, pose with their collection of Giants memorabilia.

CHAPTER 9

Why we are
the way we are

Looking Behind The Madness

Originally I thought it would be nifty to have a chapter in the book with contributions from players, coaches and othe prominent people. In talking with everyone from the players to a sociologist and a psychologist, this chapter rapidly evolved into an explanation of why we do what we do.

If you stop laughing at the crazy stories and start to thin about them, you begin to wonder why people do these things. How can someone be late for their wedding becaus the game went into overtime? How can someone endure th pain of kidney stones without seeking medical attention un after the game?

In general, how can people do things they would never d under different circumstances? This question became the focus for this chapter, "Why we are the way we are" and I' proud to present viewpoints from a wide diversity of peopl and disciplines. I think you'll find them stimulating and fun

1

The Sociology of Giants Fans

After hearing about Dr. Michael Givant (Department of Sociology, Adelphi University) and his research project involving Giants fans, I talked Dr. Givant into writing a piece for the book on some of the sociological reasons behind our behavior. What he has found, which will be part of a book he is writing, is fascinating and revealing.

In 1982, I interviewed approximately 55 Giants football fans to see if I could determine why people would "stick with a loser". I interviewed 30 fans who watched the Giants primarily on television. I also went to the Giants Stadium parking lot for the 1982 home opener against Atlanta. I got there before the parking lot opened and found two cars there with early morning fans there. By game time, I had spoken to over 20 more fans.

Despite some attempts to stop, I'd been a Giants fan for 26 years—since I was 14. I knew, all too well, the Giants record and their folklore, but not their fans. At times, I wondered if the Giants would get to the playoffs before I was pensioned off. Being a Giants fan I knew was a life sentence.

As a result of my research, I have little doubt that many of "us" will be tottering ancients telling new born generations of youngsters how we beat the Bears in the '56 title game; how we lost to the Colts in sudden death in '58 and how a bald headed messiah, with initials instead of a first name, threw often and threw deep and took us to the NFL title game three years in a row. Some of us (not myself) will recall how we walked in off the street and sat in the bleachers for 75 cents in the '56 championship game, and how we haven't been able to get a ticket since then. Many of us were teenagers, when we became fans in the Giants "glory years".

Why are "we" the way we are? My research cannot fully answer that question, but it may provide some interesting insights. Most of those with whom I spoke had become fans at sometime between eight and fourteen years old. Several seemed to have become fans even earlier. One young fan in her twenties couldn't remember when she became a fan. She said "it's in my blood". Very few people seemed to become Giants fans after age fourteen.

It is one thing to grow up watching the Giants; it is another to grow into adulthood and middle age still watching them; and in the case of real die-hard fans, to plan Sunday, if not the whole week, around being in front of the television or at the stadium. Many fans can tell stories about weddings and other social engagements which would have deterred lesser fans from watching their team, but which were simply obstacles to be surmounted by them.

How can fans "stick with a loser" for so long? For some, growing up with a winner was an integral part. The Giants experienced just two winning seasons from 1964 to 1982. Yet, they have sold out Yankee Stadium, Shea Stadium, the Yale Bowl and now Giants Stadium.

When I asked fans how they could stick with the team for so long, I found that they had a difficult time explaining. "That's a good question," one fan told me, not really sure why he watched week after week. Some described it as similar to being a member of an ethnic group—it was likened to being Irish, Italian and Jewish. People frequently told me that they were Giants fans because of "loyalty" or "they're a New York-New Jersey" team.

A few people told me that they'd be crazy not to go to games, and one fan told me he and his buddies would be there even if there were no game! I was not surprised to find that fans had a difficult time readily putting into words why they had remained fans through the years despite the Giants having lost so often and so badly.

Early in my research I found out that many of those with whom I spoke had literally grown up watching the Giants with a "significant other", usually their fathers, on Sunday afternoons. One fan told me that Sunday family dinner was planned around the ritual of watching the Giants. Another with whom I spoke said that the Giants were like part of the family. Many of those I spoke with seemed to have identified at very early ages with ritually watching the Giants.

116

When we say that Giants fans identified watching the Giants with their fathers, we mean that there is a very strong and positive sense of closeness and warmth associated with watching the Giants with one's father. To turn off the Giants would be, in a manner of speaking, akin to rejecting dad. This results in a sense of warmth and identification with the team.

That identification with the team is sometimes carried over to the players who become heroes. Several fans poignantly and painfully recalled a newspaper picture of Y.A. Tittle, dazed and bleeding, on his knees after being sacked by a Pittsburgh lineman in 1964. It was his last season and the year we fell from grace in the standings.

What do we mean when we say that something is a ritual activity? We mean that the activity is done at a set time and place. We also mean that the doing may very probably be just as important or even more important than what is being done. Rituals may evoke and maintain memories of youth, family, neighborhoods and friends. In a sense, rituals remind us of our personal histories.

Rituals also are not easily broken or forgotten when they are based on powerful childhood experiences and family activities. Like preferences for ethnic foods, they are an acquired taste which may become so much a part of ourselves that we may have no easy way of explaining why we like them so much.

As we get older, we may transfer the feeling of identification from family to friends and peers who are fellow long-suffering Giants fans. This may be especially true for those who have tickets and go to games, making a ritual of "tailgating".

Many of those with whom I spoke do not have tickets but schedule their week so they will be in front of the television at kickoff time on Sunday. Watching the weekly game may be done with friends or family. There are also personal rituals to help deal with the tension and nervous excitement that a game may provoke—sitting in a certain seat if the team is ahead, wearing a certain piece of clothing or smoking certain cigarettes. If they believe magic helps to win games, Giants fans will practice it.

Many fans expressed their long term suffering and resilient hopes. The Giants, like Sysphus' boulder, seemed to dash these hopes anew each season. Many expressed the comedy, the tragedy, the hope and the frustration of remaining a Giants fan. One man told me that he had tried to stop being a fan but was unable.

Giants fans have often expressed their anger and frustration over losing—loudly, vocally and directly. They have burned their tickets and hired an airplane which flew over the Meadowlands trailing a banner which read "15 years of lousy football". One fan told me very poignantly that Giants fans might burn their tickets but they wouldn't give away those tickets.

Why haven't "we" given up on the Giants? Do you know any ex-Giants fans? I don't. That is not to say some don't exist. It is probably easier, however, to change one's citizenship, one's spouse or one's job than it is to become an ex-Giants fan!

Many of those with whom I spoke are long term Giants fans, and were there before pro football was "discovered" by television. One old timer told me quite simply that he had grown up with the Giants: "So what are you going to do, root for another team?" (because ours is losing). It makes sense—you can't get another father—you've got to love or hate the one you have. Accordingly, if you grew up with the Giants, you may not really have any other choice!

I had come to believe that the Giants might not win this year or next year, but some day in the distant future they would win. This is what I call the "Santa Claus Syndrome". It is the hope and belief that children have even when they know there is no Santa Claus, that the mythical gift giver will appear again.

One man who became a fan in 1936 when he was 9 years old, told me that even through all the "lousy" years, he couldn't watch another team. "When you're a Giants fan, you're a Giants fan" he told me. Although my research didn't deal with it, I believe that the losing years may have, ironically, solidified some fans' loyalty.

Adversity can make a group more cohesive than it was when there was no adversity. Anyone can stay with a winner —while the team is winning. The resolve of those who remain fans during the bad times can be greatly strengthened by those bad times.

The next time you suffer through a particularly tough loss and wonder how you can ever do it again, think of it as acting out a symbolic ritual family activity.

There is, however, one indignity that we have not suffered that we no doubt will suffer when we start to win again. We will encounter the "camp followers" who like being with a winner and the "closet" fans who weren't there in the bad old days. But they'll never know how good it felt to beat Philadelphia in Philadelphia in the playoffs!

Ode to Big Blue

A couple of seasons ago, Gene McNevin's son gave him an engraved placque, which carried the following lament of a Giants fan. The author, unknown, answered the eternal question, "How can you remain so loyal to that team?" It is totally unedited; and if the author reads this book, I'd sure love to hear from him.

I am a GIANT fan

I was baptized in the waters of victory at the Cathedral of the Polo Grounds. My childhood in the days when people still burned leaves on cold, autumn Sunday afternoons was of pride in the companionship of Strong, Gifford, Rote, Conerly and Y.A. Tittle.

I am a Giant Fan.

Six days a week are the interminable boredom that prefaces the real part of life; Sunday 2PM kickoff. It is in its own way a spiritual experience; good guys dressed in vestments of Blue and Red against bad guys on an altar of green, guarded by evil high priests in black and white shirts.

I am in the trenches, helmet-to-helmet with monsters not as fierce as I. Casting aside linebackers as if they were anemic Raggedy Anns, I blindside the quarterback, strip him of the ball, and lie there with my prize as the thunder of cheering swells into every pore. I am the Walter Mitty of the Meadowlands. I have known good days and bad. I have sat through Sunday afternoons that lasted a generation.

I am a Giant fan.

I have weathered the long seasons and walked back through the parking lot with disgust as my only companion.

My anger at defeat or team apathy is legend. Often I have mentally planned the assassination of head coaches or filed a class action suit against an entire offensive line, charging malpractice.

The echo of my boos of frustration can be heard in the suburbs of hell and in Mara's executive offices. My screaming expletives have the color of a Picasso painting when a 20-yard field goal is missed. I can split an infinitive and pencil in a four-letter profanity when I see a half-hearted effort in the secondary.

I am a Giant Fan.

But I have another side to me. It is the first cousin to Love and the brother of an eternal spring that casts out the devils of too many winters of discontent. It is Hope, it is Faith. It is always Fidelity. It is 76,000 strong, and with the encouragement of a completed pass or, praise the Lord, a victory. It sends up to the heavens, cheering and elation that would make a Notre Dame home crowd sound like a soft hum of a sparrow.

I am a Giant Fan.

What Is A Giants Fan?

By Dave Klein
The Star-Ledger

What is a Giants fan? What makes an otherwise normal, well-adjusted, responsible, adult, mature person do the things Giants fans do?

Chances are no one will ever know. But let's try.

See, there are guys who go to work all week, who discuss things like interest rates and lines of credit, speak computer language and deal with decimal points in an amount that could give a healthy person palpitations. They sell show tickets or they sell cars. They advise presidents of other corporations on how to spend money. They buy stocks and hope they've made the right choice. They order "paper deliveries" of pork bellies and soybean, of all things.

Boring, right?

You bet.

So then on Sunday they can escape. They can become just like Everyman out there in the street. They can yell and scream and curse and drink and say such entertaining things as "blitz" and "screen" and "where's the damned zone support?" and "trap the end, dammit" and all the rest of those delightful football expressions that would lead the uninitiated to believe World War III had suddenly become a spectator sport.

They escape into football. In this area of the world, since our college football is limited to Rutgers and Princeton, they gravitate to the Giants. An institution . . . with fans who might lead others to believe that they, too, are in urgent need of an institution.

It wasn't always thus. Back in the 1920's and 1930's, the Mara family tried in vain to GIVE AWAY tickets. Right, give 'em away. Nobody cared. There was Notre Dame then, and Army, and Fordham, and NYU . . . and besides, what the hell was pro football?

Things have changed dramatically.

They did so because it became "in" to be at Giants games, but only after the elite class of New York (which, in truth, once had an elite class) was sure the Giants would win more often than they lost. After all, losing is boring. Anyone can lose. Why would someone rich and powerful and wealthy and educated align himself with a losing team?

So they became Giants fans, mostly in 1956, when the team had the double good sense not only to move from the Polo Grounds to Yankee Stadium (being asssociated with the New York Yankees, pre-Steinbrenner, was good), but to win the National Football League championship, in a 47–7 rout of George Halas and his Chicago Bears.

And suddenly it was the thing to do on a Sunday afternoon. Only on Sunday afternoon, it should be noted, because major network television, Monday nights and Howard the Mouth hadn't been visited upon the struggling NFL yet.

They'd show up in their furs and top hats, sometime around the middle of the second quarter. Then they'd leave, sometime in the middle of the third quarter, having seen their friends and having had sufficient time to make plans for dinner.

But the real people, who will forever desire to emulate the rich and popular, needed some additional time before they could find a way to secure the tickets. Then, presto!, the Giants became Everyman's favorite team, too. And you know what? Everyman found out he liked pro football. Like it? He loved it. He became addicted to Robustelli and Huff, Webster and Gifford, Rote and Brown, Landry and Grier, Conerly and Shofner and Walton and Katcavage and Modzelewski and Patton and . . . .well, you get the idea.

The Golden Age of the New York Giants probably started in the middle 1950's and continued through the early part of the 1960's, a decade's worth of glory and success that confirmed what the fans had anticipated for the decade prior and cemented the inexplicable loyalty that remains now, even though 20 years of impossibly lousy football just now seems to be diminishing.

Why do Giants fans act the way they do? Because now it's habit, an addiction more insidious than narcotics, almost as if the Maras were Svengalis in modern dress.

Through three "home stadiums" until Giants Stadium . . . from Yankee Stadium to the Yale Bowl to Shea Stadium . . . the fans stayed. Through ice storms and blizzards, they stayed. Through some of the most depressingly incompetent seasons, they stayed.

They stayed when the team drafted Rocky Thompson instead of Jack Tatum . . . when it drafted Wayne Walton instead of Phil Villapiano . . . when it traded away the rights to Randy White in order to acquire quarterback Craig Morton.

They stayed, and many of the sportswriters who have stayed with the team for many, many years are still puzzled, at a loss to say why they have stayed.

But the question of loyalty has never been raised.

"My husband," says one football widow, "should be as loyal to me as he is to those damned Giants."

Aha! That, indeed, is another subject for another day.

Those Distant Giants Fans

By Jack Shepherd

The true test of the loyalty of a Giants Football Team fan comes in direct proportion to that fan's distance from the 50-yard line at East Rutherford. The greater the distance, the greater the test.

122

Some Giants fans think their loyalty is tested by having to sit, Sunday after Sunday, up high and far, far away from the 50, at the stadium. Others declare themselves loyal Giants fans because they live out of the Greater New York area, and take the shuttle into LaGuardia, a bus into Manhattan and another bus to New Jersey for the game.

I started as a Giants fan while I was a graduate student at Columbia University. That was in 1960, and I have been a Giants fan ever since despite these facts: I have only seen the team play once; I don't own a television set, and therefore listen to the games on the radio; I have moved from New York City, traveled as a journalist around the world, and now reside in northern New England.

While a graduate student, I played touch football in Riverside Park on Sunday mornings, and then huddled next to the radio, hushing my bored new wife, listening to the Giants win—as they usually did in the early 1960's—in nearby Yankee Stadium. When I started traveling a lot as a Senior Editor for Look Magazine, I would check for Giants scores in odd places like the International Herald Tribune, or the Addis Ababa Herald or the Nairobi Nation. If, as often happened, the score didn't appear until Tuesday or Wednesday, or not at all—I noticed a certain rise in my level of anxiety.

But these were good days, in more ways than one, and the Giants won a lot, lost a few, and made the names Shofner, Tittle, Webster and even Koy household words—in the places I stayed, at least—from Grenada to Tanzania.

The Giants "died" a few years before Look Magazine. I suspect that historians and anthropologists, looking back over these ruins, will see in Tittle's end zone injury at Yankee Stadium the beginning of the end. I can still see the photograph of Y.A. on his knees, just inside the goal line, as clearly as though I were now standing—as I had been—at the Federal Palace Hotel in Lagos, Nigeria, when I first saw it.

Let's omit the 1970's—mercifully. Like Tittle in that photograph, frozen forever on his knees, head bowed, injured, the Giants remained (for me) frozen in time.

Still, I continued searching out their scores in newspapers in San Francisco, and on an aircraft carrier off North Vietnam. Now, however, the news was bad, and getting worse. "Eldridge Small?" I shouted at friends in London when I heard the news. "Rocky Thompson!" I gasped at natives in Ethiopia. "Who's he?" I confess that I argued forcefully in Amsterdam that Al Simpson was going to turn the franchise around.

There were moments of surprising discovery. While interviewing Ogden Reid for a story that never ran in The New York Times Sunday Magazine, I had dinner, the evening of the NFL draft, with the Reid family in their elegant Washington, DC home. The conversation was going slowly until, during the main course, one of their young sons rushed in and shouted to everyone: "We got Van Pelt!! We got Van Pelt!!" The rest of the evening turned to the essential national issues: Could an all-America Michigan cornerback become a successful NFL linebacker? As things turned out, Van Pelt did better than that.

As a freelance author, I began writing books at home during the early 1970's. I remember writing The Adams Chronicles during the hot summer of 1975, and listening to the Giants pre-season games on WNEW. The big debate that summer around my house was not whether or not John Quincy Adams was an outstanding Secretary of State and a lousy President, but whether Martin should play tight end and who would be the quarterback.

Moving to Vermont proved traumatic in many ways. We had lived for 16 years in Manhattan and left friends, neighbors, a lovely brownstone—and excellent reception of Giants games. Our first home, south of Burlington, was a quarter-mile from our mailbox, two miles from a paved road and light years from news about the Giants. To sustain myself, I drove 15 miles into Burlington as often as I could to read The New York Times at the library (other city papers never made it into Vermont).

We moved to Norwich in 1977. Now, I get the Times every day in a little slot at our charming country store. When the newspaper is missing, which it sometimes is, I feel the old Addis Ababa anxiety rising. Did the Giants trade Jeter? Who's going to play tight end this year?

Worst—or best—of all, I listen to the Giants on the radio. On cloudy Sundays, WNEW reaches me faintly; otherwise, I have to get in my car, and drive to the top of the hill behind my house, where, motor running, I can barely hear the game.

It reminds me of summers in New Jersey, listening at night to the Brooklyn Dodgers, with a storm making "Red" Barber's voice fade in and out. I am somehow content sitting in the car, looking out across the Vermont hills, hearing a faint distant voice: ". . . the pass is in the air . . . Woolfolk makes a sensational one-handed . . . " Now, that's an experience!

****

Jack Shepherd is a noted journalist and author of nine books, among them many best sellers. I'm pleased he took time out to reminisce about his last 23 years as a Giants fan.

Giants Players Tell It Like It Is!

I had an opportunity to visit the Giants during minicamp in May, and spent some time talking with the players about the fans. The overwhelming response was that Giants fans are a step above all others in the league. Brad Van Pelt said, "By far, they're the best fans in the NFL. Whether they cheer or boo, they do it because they care."

Roy Simmons put it another way: "We don't see this inspiration anywhere else in the NFL—the fans defend us and stand up for us." Harry Carson spells Giants fans "L-O-Y-A-L" and admires the way they stick with the team, year after year.

Tom Mullady views the fans as "extremely supportive" and wants to be a part of the winning tradition. Brad Benson says "The fans give us an edge on the field. We'd love to get the Super Bowl not only for ourselves, but for the fans, who really deserve and would appreciate it more than anyone else." Floyd Eddings says "They really fire me up . . . they love to see great things happen."

Almost every player mentioned the supportiveness of the fans, especially through the lean years. Larry Heater: "Once a Giants fan . . . always a Giants fan." Gordon King said, "It's great when they're behind us . . . it's permanent loyalty." Joe Danelo recalled the Dallas game in which his field goals forced overtime and later won the game. "The encouragement from the fans helped me through that game. They could have booed after I missed early on, but they didn't. They stuck with me and it paid off."

The fans also appreciate the nature of the Giants fans. Beasley Reece: "We get a more sophisticated crowd . . . lots of nice ladies and gentlemen enjoying the game." Johnny Perkins puts it very simply, "We get the best turnout," and from Scott Brunner, "It's great to play before such a crowd, one that's educated about the game."

The word "most" popped up often: Rob Carpenter, Jeff Baldinger and Bruce Kimball said, respectively, that the Giants fans were "the most vocal, the most enthusiastic and the most faithful." Billy Ard: "It's the best place in the NFL to play, especially when we're winning!" Mike Whittington noted that "The fans are behind us all the time," and from Larry Flowers: "We love playing for the home fans."

Danny Pittman thinks the fans are "A really great group of people who give us a psychological lift," and Ernie Hughes calls it "inspirational motivation . . . a little bit of the killer instinct . . . gets our adrenalin going."

Sylvester McGrew hasn't seen anything else like it, and Brian Carpenter thinks the fans are a "wild, crazy bunch."

The coaches feel the same way: Ron Erhardt says "The fans make things exciting . . . their loyalty is amazing. New coach Tom Bresnahan says, "I hear the fans are unbelievable here!"

New head coach Bill Parcells traces his Giants roots back to his days as a youngster, when he watched Channel 5 TV's "Giants Quarterback Huddle" with Marty Glickman. He has witnessed fan behavior all over the country, and "Giants fans have a much greater percentage of hard-core, non-deviating loyalty than most other fans. I've received a tremendous amount of support from everyone, and we look forward to a great year."

View From The Family

In several recent interviews with Giants management, a particularly positive picture emerged in terms of their feelings about Giants fans. The loyalty of the fans is something the Mara family, and the rest of the Giants management, cherishes dearly. They've seen other franchises turn their backs on fans, raise ticket prices and so forth. And while winning seasons have been scarce until recently, local fans can see a change in the spirit and manner in which the Giants are planning for the future.

Against this backdrop, we talked at length about the reasons behind our loyalty, and came up with a social/ tradition/identity pattern. Tom Power, Director of Publicity, says, "It goes back to the great years . . . to the Conerly's, Rotes, Tittles and Shofners. They originally established a following, and then after that it became a social event. People would come every week, sit in the same seats, get to know the people around them. They grew up together and shared each other's life experiences. First they might have started out single, then got married and had kids. With each passing year they would get more seats in the same section for their families. And they would see their friends at the game, and look forward to sharing. During the championship years, it was an extremely positive experience, and when things went downhill, they stuck with us."

The ability of the fans to stick with the Giants during the 18 years seems to be a result of carrying the tradition around, knowing that someday it will return in all its glory. Power: "Our fans are unique . . . their loyalty is unmatched . . . nobody stays with a team like the Giants do."

Ed Croke, Director of Media Services, views the situation as part of birthright. "Most of us are born into a political party, a religion and most of us are born into being a Giants fan! If they move from one end of the country to the other, they're still Giants fans. Every place we go . . . every city we play in . . . we wind up with Giants fans."

Adds GM George Young, "They materialize wherever we go. The New York area is a big training ground, from which people get transferred all over the country . . . but they retain their loyalty to the Giants."

All of the letters received by Power, Croke, Young and the Mara family all start off the same way: "I've been a loyal Giants fan since 1930. And I want to discuss the draft . . . ." Young gets letters from people he figures out to be well over 60 years old: "These guys have been Giants fans since I was six years old!"

As we see more and more evidence of Giants management striving to put a Super Bowl team on the field, you begin to realize that the bad years are over, that management does indeed respect and value the fans' loyalty immensely. The feeling, both in the stands and in the front offices is that the Giants are on their way!

A Mass Altered State

In a conversation with psychologist Dr. Elaine Eden, many possible reasons for our unique behavior patterns were examined. Taken separately, they are most interesting. But put together, they paint a vivid picture of the mind of the Giants fan—one which is a rich combination of many different and creative psychological 'personalities', if you will.

Dr. Eden offers many possible distinct reasons for our over-aggressive and self-sacrificing behavior patterns, which exist only for this team and probably not in any other event in our lives.

One is that the Giants game is an escape from reality, a chance to block out personal and family problems, and put aside world hunger, nuclear war and other major concerns. Much in the same way 'Raiders of the Lost Ark' offered a couple of hours of an escape from reality, so does forming an alliance with this team. You know that every Sunday there's a game which puts you in another world. Whether you're successful or are loaded with problems, the game is a change of pace, and it gives you the ability and privilege of acting differently than you normally do.

Most of us want to be very successful, to be winners, but few achieve that goal. Therefore, many people over-identify with the Giants, a group of athletes struggling to win. People tend to put all their fantasies of success onto the team, and therefore are unbelievably ecstatic when the Giants win and undeniably morose when they lose. Perhaps this accounts for a larger thrill coming from a Giants victory or 52 yard TD than from a promotion or major sale.

Being at the game, with the beer, the noise, the weather and the crowd makes it easy for us to act like little boys and girls. Life was simple back then—all you cared about was who won the game. Beat the other guys was all that mattered. Taxes, jobs and other problems never existed at that age. Reverting back to childhood is healthy, something we all should do; the atmosphere at the game allows the little child in us all to feel free. As informal surveys show, this indeed is the case.

There's also something Dr. Eden calls a 'mass altered state' which exists at the games. It happens in other sports but not nearly as regularly as it does at Giants games, where the feeling is that everyone is brethren. A good example was the olympic ice hockey game when the US beat Russia. Everyone in the country identified with Pavelich, Johnson and company against the big red machine.

It's the same with Giants fans—we're all in the same boat—and we would do anything for each other. The response of fans in submitting articles for this book was a good example of being caught up in what can only be described as 'a cause'.

This mass altered state, one whereby people, at the drop of a hat, become hypnotized with Giants fever, actually might have some physiological and chemical basis. Just as falling in love does have chemical components, so does being in love with the Giants—many a football wife would verify their husbands actually love the team!

The forces when people enter this state of mind are very strong, causing them to do things they would never do in 'real life'—paying $200 for a ticket or slugging it out with someone over a ref's call.

What happens is that the 'high' one gets is so high that it blocks out everything that is sane. And the anticipation of this weekly high causes unusual behavior during the days preceding the game.

As we'll all readily admit to being Giants fanatics, we explored the definition and characteristics of fanatical behavior. The typical definition of fanatic went like this: "a person whose behavior results from possession by a demon". Well, the demon in this case is whatever each individual needs—escape from reality, identification with a team, and so forth.

Fanaticism is something quoted by many, but this phrase by Winston Churchill sums it up best: "A fanatic is one who can't change his mind and won't change the subject."

As a psychological summary, feel free to categorize your behavior as any or all of the following:

(1) Rooting for the Giants is an escape from reality.
(2) The Giants enable us to identify with a group struggling to win.
(3) The mood at the Games frees us to act like little kids, to regress to our childhoods.
(4) The mass appeal and state of mind acts as a hypnotic trance.
(5) We become possessed by a force which lasts before, during and after the game.

Now that we've uncovered the deep, dark reasons behind our eccentricities, do you think that will change anything? Heck no!

Dave Jennings

I caught up with Dave a few months back and asked him about Giants fans. His feelings, I think, are shared by most of the players.

"When we go out there every Sunday on the field, they're (the fans) are all there. It's great to have this kind of backing. In other stadiums, the people just aren't there; once we went to Buffalo and only 17,000 people were in the stands. We know the people behind our bench and say hello to them each week."

"Our fans are honest . . . and forgiving. They let us know when they don't like what we're doing, but they support us unlike any other team's fans. And there's always Giants fans at away games . . . they always sit together and we get the feeling there's a mini-Giants stadium when we play on the road. It's great when you're in a strange hotel somewhere and people come up to you and say they're Giants fans."

Dave Jennings loves the fans, the Giants and being a part of a family that extends past the players, coaches and management into the stands.

Around The League

I received a very interesting analysis of Giants fans when compared to those of other teams, and part of the reasoning behind Charles Nash's explanation lies in the nature of the New York metropolitan area itself.

This area, he argues, "has always been noted for its fast paced lifestyle. People of this region take their jobs seriously. They take their play seriously too. And they take the Giants seriously."

"Metropolitan man can block out all superflous distractions and think of just one thing—the game. They do not want cheerleaders, halftime shows or freebies at the gate. They want no banners to obstruct the view of people behind them. Watching Giant football is a complete sadistic manifestation, something man of this area has been conditioning himself for all of his life."

Keeping this background in mind, Charles takes a look at the fans of other clubs.

DALLAS COWBOYS

Cowboy fans take pride in their cheerleaders. Giants fans go to the game to watch the Giants, not the girls.

WASHINGTON REDSKINS

Redskins fans are pretty good, but they are transient. They come and go every four or six years, whenever their team is up. Also, they have that dreadful band, that only plays one song. The Giants don't need a band.

ST. LOUIS CARDINALS

St. Louis Cardinal fans may not exist. They do not show up for the games. Giants fans show up for every game, and come from over 10 different states.

PHILADELPHIA EAGLES

Though they are good fans, they are more involved with themselves than their team. They are loud because they want to boost their ego and keep the broadcasters believing that they are the most hostile. Giants fans do not undress in the winter.

PITTSBURGH STEELERS

Steeler fans crawled out of the mines and factories and brought their linens with them. A plethora of terrible towels and horrible hankies pervaded their championships. Steeler fans seem as if they were more interested in their accouterments rather than their team.

MIAMI DOLPHINS

The Dolphins are the originators of hanky waving. The only thing I ever saw a Giant fan wave was a ten dollar bill disguised under an old ticket at the entrance gate.

NEW YORK JETS

Jet fans are sort of like Giants fans' little brothers. They do not have cheerleaders—good. They watch the game intently—good. They do, however, resort to instant violence—bad—when things don't go their way.

HOUSTON OILERS

A game in the dome contains the regalia of a high school or college game. With all the pom poms in the air, how can you see the game?

LOS ANGELES RAIDERS

These fans had a good time admiring their silver and black heroes puncture lungs for years. Despite good seasons, the witnessing of this assault has taken its toll. The Raider fan is so confused that he now attends games played in the spring, and roots for a team that wears yellow and blue!

Giants fans fill up the stadium every week, and it's easy to see why other teams don't. There is something special about this team, this stadium, this area, this heritage.

CHAPTER 10

Giants general store: resources.

Roast A Giant!

The Valerie Fund is a very special organization, dedicated to raising funds for "cancer research and care for children and their families." Every year, they have a special charity sports banquet roast, featuring Giants players, coaches and management. It's a wonderful time, put on by all volunteers.

Ed Goldstein coordinates the event, which has featured Bill Parcells, "The Crunch Bunch", Dave Klein of The Star Ledger, Dave Jennings, Phil Simms, George Young, J.T. Turner, and in days gone by, Larry Csonka, Jim Kiick and Don Shula.

It's always a heartwarming night, with dinner and the roast at a different site each year, with all proceeds benefitting the clinic fund which operates at Overlook Hospital in Summit, New Jersey. The fund also puts out a newsletter, and details may be obtained from the address below.

VALERIE FUND
40 Somerset Street
Plainfield NJ 07060
(201) 647–6688

The Football Giants Fan Club

Representing and Uniting Giants Fans Since 1969

Henry DeBianchi is a die-hard Giants fan. So is his new bride, Nancy. Together, they've been cutting, pasting, writing, editing and mailing THE GIANT, the official publication of The Football Giants Fan Club, of which Henry is president.

Henry founded the club in 1969 when he was barely 16 years old! What developed from a teenage passion was a club of Giants fans encompassing 27 states, Canada, France, England, Japan and West Germany!

Club members regularly contribute their comments, and vote on the "best" and "worst" football coverage, announcers, and so forth. They annually select the offensive, defensive and most valuable players each year. They also have an away game trip, day at training camp, and an annual banquet, with players and coaches in attendance. For a membership brochure, write:

Henry DeBianchi
The Football Giants Fan Club
28 Cleveland Avenue
Waldwick NJ 07463
(201) 444–9638

New York Giants Fan Club Of New England

When Mitch Goodhue and his buddies get toghether to go to the Giants games these days, the driveway must look like the parking lot of Giants stadium. Between the group, their boast the largest collection of Giants license plates: GIANT, GIANT 3, NYGF, GIANT 5, GIANT 7. The group travels from outside Boston, and has been since the early 70's to most every home game. They've also been flying to many away games, including the wonderful victory over the Eagles a couple of years back. Ken Hartford had to take a $250 loan just to get there! Between the core of the group, over $1,000 is spent each year on their Giants fanatacism.

They've taken a camper down to some of the games with 8 or 10 guys. They've been stuck at small airports in the middle of nowhere due to bad weather en route to Giants games.

Says Malden Ron Anderson, "The Giants are our lives. We are almost members of a cult. If someone came down during halftime and said 'if you drink this stuff the Giants would win', we would, even if we knew it was cyanide!"

Ron every once in a while has the following exchange with his wife: "Every once in a while she gets fed up and she tells me I love football more than her. I tell her, 'but I love you more than basketball.'"

Founded in 1974, the club has over 250 members, and they put out about 4 newsletters called "Giants News" each year. They get together annually (aside from the games) for a party at which they eat, drink and talk nothing but Giants football. Dues are $2.50 per year. Write:

New York Giants Fan Club of New England
Box 17
East Walpole MA 02032

The Kickoff Club

According to its President Tom Scott, THE KICKOFF CLUB is a group of small businessmen and executives who started meeting in 1958 when the Giants were king.

The membership has grown over the years to about 100, and Tom indicates new members are welcome. They meet seven times per year in the TrophyRoom at Gallagher's Restaurant, six during the regular season and on St. Patrick's day.

All their meetings are luncheons, and Giants players usually address the group; plus their are football related door prizes.

"All in all, we're a bunch of successful people who are really dedicated to the Giants. It's a wonderful way of getting together."

For further information, write:

> **Tom Scott**
> **The Kickoff Club**
> **Post Office Box 1937**
> **New York NY 10017**
> **Phone 212–486–5750**

140

Giant Boosters of Bergen County

This closely knit group of avid Giants fans not only attends every Giants home game, but travels around the country in pursuit of the blue. But in addition, the club plans and runs many fund raising activities for charitable causes, and proudly has Giants players and staff in attendance.

Founded in 1974 by Fiore Paluscio, the boosters attend every home game and travel to many away contests. They were a section of "blue" in a sea of orange in San Francisco for the playoff game. The group represent a bunch of hard working people who love the Giants, and love being able to make a contribution to various charities, hospitals and worthwhile causes.

Hats off to the Giant Boosters of Bergen County . . . another proud member of the Giants family!

THE **GIANTS** NEWSWEEKLY

This lively, colorful newspaper covers the Giants in depth and is published 28 times per year, weekly from August through to the end of the season, and monthly during the off-season.

Each issue contains exclusive action photographs, Coach Bill Parcells' analysis, General Manager George Young's question-and-answer column, plus regular columnists Dave Klein (The Star-Ledger), Vinny DiTrani (The Bergen Record), Bruce Lowitt (Associated Press), Dave Solomon (New Haven Journal-Courier).

The Giants Newsweekly also features comprehensive statistical analysis, game stories and more. An annual subscription is $19.95; two years is $36.95. For further information, write:

Giants Newsweekly
P.O. Box 816
Red Bank NJ 07701
(201) 747–1085

Inside Football®

FOR THE BEST INFORMED GIANT FAN

This publication is actually a newsletter, covering the Giants in considerable depth. Inside Giants Football looks to analyze the team, its players and coaches, in a behind-the-scenes look, delving into the issues behind the decisions.

Inside Giants Football publishes 20 weekly issues during the season, and the yearly subscription rate is $19.50. They are offering a special free bonus for new subscribers in a report called "Analysis of Team Needs and Management Interviews".

One quotation from a subscriber sums up this publication's editorial goal: "I enjoy your game analyses and especially agree with your evaluation of the play calling." For further information, write or call:

Inside Giants Football
159 West 33rd St.
New York NY 10001
1 (800) 852–5000

New Jersey Sports Collector's Show

Twice a year, Bill Jacobowitz and Pat Gonella put on a very special show for sport's buffs. Held in convenient New Jersey hotels, the show features exhibits, vendors selling cards and other items for all sports.

They often have famous athletes who speak and sign autographs; this past spring Lawrence Taylor of 'The Crunch Bunch' was the featured guest. There are additionally door prizes, and it's a great show for sports enthusiasts. For details, write:

N.J. Sports Collector's Show
c/o Bill Jacobowitz
48 Harrison Ave.
West Orange NJ 07052
(201) 992–6919

Checklist of Giants Collectibles

No true Giants fan is without the t-shirts, mugs, helmets and other collectibles that he can buy. Some fans own a few from the checklist presented here, while others might own all of these items.

If you're planning a Giants den or exhibit room, you might use this checklist when making your purchases. Many of these items can be found at local sporting goods stores, Sears NFL center and at the stadium vendors. All of these items have the Giants distinctive red, white and blue logo on them. I've broken them down by category just in case you are organized like me.

LOOK THE PART

( ) football jersey
( ) t-shirt
( ) athletic shorts
( ) sweatshirt
( ) sweater
( ) sneakers
( ) casual shoes
( ) belt
( ) belt buckle
( ) wallet
( ) coach sweater
( ) jeans with patch
( ) sweatpants
( ) helmet stick pins
( ) calendar
( ) warm up suit
( ) socks
( ) cap

BUNDLE UP

( ) hooded sweatshirt
( ) gloves
( ) windbreaker
( ) waterproof boots
( ) jacket
( ) parka
( ) mittens

SWEET DREAMS

( ) pajamas
( ) slippers
( ) bathrobe SHOW IT OFF!
( ) ceramic mug lamp
( ) ashtray
( ) latch hook rugs
( ) afghan pillows
( ) floor mats
( ) wall placque
( ) desk organizer
( ) cork board
( ) helmet lamp
( ) wastepaper basket
( ) pencils
( ) desk lamp
( ) mirror

DRINK UP!

( ) ceramic mug
( ) beer stein
( ) tankard
( ) bar glasses

NOT IN MY BED YOU WON'T!

( ) bedspread
( ) draperies
( ) valances
( ) pillows
( ) sleeping bag
( ) sheets

EXCUSE ME . . .

( ) soap bar
( ) towel set
( ) bath towels

THE KIDS ROOM

( ) toy vans
( ) bank
( ) knapsack
( ) football cards
( ) gym bag
( ) helmet
( ) toy players
( ) toy uniforms & helmets
( ) posters
( ) pictures
( ) helmet clock
( ) watch
( ) wall clock
( ) penant

Books About The Giants

By Dave Klein

**THE NEW YORK GIANTS:
YESTERDAY, TODAY AND TOMORROW**
Regnery-Contemporary Books

THE GAME OF THEIR LIVES
Random House, Hardcover
New American Library, Paperback

GIANTS AGAIN!
New American Library, Paperback

THE PRO FOOTBALL MYSTIQUE
New American Library, Paperback

CHAPTER 11

Are you a true blue Giants fan?

Are You a True Blue Giants Fan?

Everyone claims to be the ultimate Giants fan, the #1 supporter, the most loyal, the oldest, longest, youngest, super fan. Everyone who wrote, with virtually no exceptions, believes he has done more for the 'cause' than anyone else.

A situation like that calls for a special questionnaire to determine how much of a die-hard you really are. If you answer honestly, you'll get a true picture as to the degree of your love for the Giants. You'll learn in which areas you need improvement and where you are satisfactory. In this manner, you can become a better Giants fan through learning.

If you answer dishonestly, the only one you're fooling is yourself. No one will believe you got all the right answers to these questions. What you can do is write your answers to the following questions and mail them to us. For the next edition of 'Those Crazy Giants Fans' we'll publish the results. Send your completed surveys—postcards only—to:

Those Crazy Giants Fans
Survey Department
Box 264WOB
West Orange NJ 07052

Let's get in the swing of things with an elementary example. Remember the SAT, where they make you put little marks in little boxes? Well, that's not necessary here. All you have to do is write the number of the question on a postcard, followed by a dash, and then by the letter answer to the question. For those who didn't understand what I just wrote, it looks like this:

1—B

OK, now for the sample question:

From the list of ten colors below, pick two of your favorites.

A. orange
B. purple
C. red
D. black
E. green
F. blue
G. gold
H. yellow
I. brown

At this point, you would indicate your answers on your postcard. The correct answers to this question happen to be C and F. If you picked anything but red and blue, go root for the Cowboys and don't ever show your face at Giants stadium. Not only is the cover of this book done only in red and blue, the phrases "blue wall" and "true blue" are mentioned throughout this book. Shame on you if you can't get past the sample question. For those of you who did, however, don't smirk. Things will get tough . . . we will separate the men from the boys. ARE YOU A TRUE BLUE GIANTS FAN?

Official Questions

(1) Indicate which of the following you have done or anticipate doing during the course of a football season. Exhibition games can be included.

A. Swear to see or hear every single Giants game, no matter what happens. Weddings, bad health or threats on your life are not acceptable excuses.
B. Get into at least one highly volatile if not violent encounter defending the Giants.
C. Wear a Giants hat, jersey or some article of clothing whenever viewing a game.
D. Watch highlights of all Giants victories on a minimum of three different channels.
E. Read accounts of every Giants victory in at least two different newspapers.
F. Come close to any of the following due to your vow in "A" above: divorce, separation or cold shoulder from spouse; or miss any significant portion of a wedding, Bar Mitzvah or other so-called special affair due to a conflict in scheduling.

(2) Choose the four most important items from the following list, and place them in order of importance.

A. Making love
B. Eating
C. Sleeping
D. Watching the Giants
E. Success on the job
F. Being thin
G. Reading
H. Having friends
I. Avoiding the draft
J. Living to an old age

(3) If season tickets became available, but the only way to get them was to pay $5000 for a lifetime ticket, which of the following methods of raising the cash would you choose? You can select more than one answer.

A. Get a second mortgage on your house.
B. Hoc the family car.
C. Paint the white yard lines on the football field with a toothbrush.
D. Accept an underworld contract to perform a violent crime for pay.
E. Become a soldier of fortune for a month.
F. Collect 20,000 bottles or 32 tons of newspaper for recycling.
G. Sell Girl Scout cookies (or light bulbs) door to door.
H. Peddle magazine subscriptions or sell encyclopedias.

(4) How long have you been a Giants fan?

A. Under one year
B. One to five years
C. Five to ten years
D. Ten to twenty years
E. Twenty to fifty years
F. More than fifty years
G. More than seventy five years

(5) During the time you have been a fan, how many games have you missed either seeing or hearing?

A. Zero
B. One or two
C. A handful
D. A dozen
E. About twenty
F. Close to a hundred
G. Most of them

154

(6) In the play that has come to be known as "The Fumble", list up to three of your reactions upon seeing, hearing or reading about it.

A. Throw a rock at the TV, crush the radio or burn the newspaper because you thought they were lieing.
B. Pack up and move the family to Dallas.
C. Think about suicide, torture or other means of self-inflicted pain.
D. Quit your job due to depression and answer an ad for stuffing envelopes.
E. Consider becoming a monk in a convent where TV broadcasts are prohibited.
F. Calling up your former college roommate who happens to be an Eagle fan, and offering to buy that person the most expensive dinner around.
G. Going on a hunger strike.
H. Joining the Peace Corps.
I. All of the above.
J. Other:

(7) Going down the stretch of the '81 season, with dramatic victories putting the Giants into the playoffs for the first time in eons, what were your reactions going into the San Francisco game? Select any three.

A. Prepare to go to Iran if that's where they were holding the Super Bowl.
B. Bet every single cent, including savings, insurance policy dividends, stock, gold, silver and precious gems that the Giants would make it.
C. Better than the day you got your first job.
D. Better than the first time you discovered the word 'sex'.
E. Better than 'pigging' out on all your favorite foods.
F. Better than getting a date with the Playboy/Playgirl centerfold.
G. Agree to anything your mother-in-law says if it could insure a victory.
H. Agree to any off-season demand your wife makes if it could insure a victory.
I. All of the above.
J. Others:

(8) How many (do not itemize, it's past tax time) of the following items with Giants emblems, do you own? Remember, each item must contain the official Giants logo.

A. beanie
B. cap
C. penant
D. bumper sticker
E. t-shirt
F. jersey
G. decal
H. patch
I. mug
J. blanket
K. sweatshirt
M. helmet
N. sheets
O. towels
P. key ring
Q. wall clock
R. wastepaper basket
S. calendar
T. gym bag
U. belt buckle
V. other items you have made yourself with the Giants emblem on it:
W. other items you would buy if they made them:

That's all for our official Giants survey. I hope you've enjoyed the questions, and that you'll take the time to send your answers in on a postcard. I'll tabulate the results, perform strict scientific tests such as chi square and deviation from the norm, and report back to you in the next edition.

CHAPTER 12

We want to hear from you

We Want To Hear From You!

You can probably guess what a monumental job it was putting together this book. In order to let the fans know I was working on such a project, I took out some advertisements, got some free publicity, and received much help from the Giants front office. They were able to refer me to many 'unique' Giants fans.

The response was great, and I'm planning THOSE CRAZY GIANTS FANS, Volume II, for publication next year. If all goes well, the book should be bigger, with more stories and more pictures.

That's where you come in. Since this book is about Giants fans, I can't do it without your help. It only costs you some time and a twenty cent stamp.

Please submit any and all stories, and if we use yours, you'll get a copy of the book free of charge, with your name, story and, if possible, picture in it! It's a good deal, and knowing the dedication of Giants fans, worth your time and effort. Please—type or print.

In case you were wondering, we used 90 percent of the stories we received this time. They were all excellent, and the only reason some were left out was due to duplication.

I know among the hundreds of thousands of Giants fans in the metropolitan area, there must be thousands of more wonderful stories and photographs. Please make your submissions as early as possible, and you may submit more than one story.

For everyone that submitted a story for this edition, I thank you for your cooperation. And for the rest of you, start writing . . . after all, this is YOUR book! Send stories to:

Irv Brechner Targeted Marketing Inc.
P.O. Box 453
Livingston NJ 07039

THANK YOU!

CHAPTER 13

The author
lives out his
boyhood fantasies.

A Dream Come True!

I'd venture to say that everyone of us has dreamt, at some time or another, to be out on the field at Giants Stadium, dressed up in a Giants uniform, scoring touchdowns, kicking extra points and tackling would be runners.

For my brother Howie and myself, that dream came true one crisp, cool May morning (felt more like September).

We were met bright and early by Tom Power, the Giants PR Director, who had arranged for us to take photographs for about an hour. Here we were, two die-hard fans being treated like one of the team. We were led down through the caverns under the stands, where we could hear the echoes of great Giants victories.

We were met at the locker room by the Wagner family— Ed, Pat and Ed Jr.—who outfitted us from head to toe. We first got into our "grays"—the gray shirt and shorts you wear under the uniform.

Ed Jr. then fitted two of the smallest sets of shoulder pads on us (we're both 5'7", 155 lbs), which later took ten minutes to get off. Next we struggled to get the jerseys over our pads (there must be a trick). While we were lacing up our spankling white new shoes, Ed brought us our pants, complete with pads. Well, we finally were dressed, and trotted down the hall to the tunnel, the sounds of our cleats beating a steady ryhthm (we didn't wear metal cleats, but that sounded good, didn't it?).

To the cheers of 73,000 fans, we burst out on the field, holding our Giants helmets high, looking like what we've always dreamed about. The announcer told the fans who we were and where we went to college, and our pictures flashed on the screen. You must have guessed by now that the stands were empty, there was no announcer, and Howie, myself and the photographer were the only ones on the field. But that's not the way it felt.

What follows is a pictorial of the wonderful hour we spent on the field, pretending to be Giants players. Linda Bohm, our photographer, and her assistant Bernadette, spent a chilly 60 minutes in the wind and cold, changing film, setting up tripods, and doing all the good things photographers do. The time and effort was well worth it. I think you'll enjoy it.

Introducing, numbers 34 and 38, the tandem backfield out of Franklin & Marshall and Seton Hall, tailbacks Howard and Irv Brechner . . .

Blue 97 . . . blue 97 . . . three sixteen . . . three sixteen . . . hut, hut, hut.

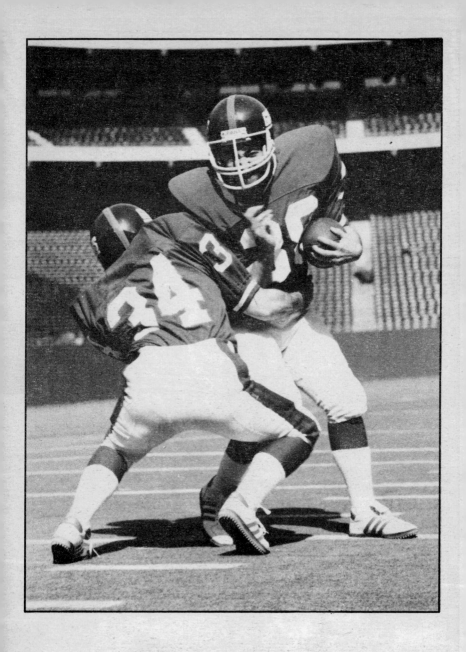

Brechner is brought down on after busting up the middle for a 12 yard gain.

Howard Brechner, all alone in the secondary, pulls it in . . . another spectacular grab! QB Irv Brechner (inset), fades back to pass . . .

**High five in the end zone as the Brechners
team up for another TD.**

Brechner goes high in the end zone, about to spike the ball, after that miraculous catch off the 49 yard pass play.

The ball is snapped, placed down and kicked
. . . it's high enough, has the distance . . . and
it's good!

1983 GIANTS SCHEDULE

DAY/DATE	HOME or AWAY	BROADCAST TIME	OPPONENT	TV CBS CH. 2	TV NBC CH. 4	TV ABC CH. 7	TV WPIX CH. 11	RADIO WNEW 1130 AM
8/7 SUNDAY	H	12 MID	New York Jets (Exhibition)				X	X
		8 PM						X
8/12 FRIDAY	A	8 PM	Pittsburgh Steelers (Exhibition)			X		X
8/20 SATURDAY	H	12 MID	Baltimore Colts (Exhibition)				X	
		8 PM						X
8/26 FRIDAY	H	12 MID	Miami Dolphins (Exhibition)				X	
		8 PM						X
9/4 SUNDAY	H	1 PM	Los Angeles Rams	X				X
9/11 SUNDAY	A	1 PM	Atlanta Falcons	X				X
9/18 SUNDAY	A	2 PM	Dallas Cowboys	X				X
9/26 MONDAY	H	9 PM	Green Bay Packers			X		X
10/2 SUNDAY	H	4 PM	San Diego Chargers		X			X
10/9 SUNDAY	H	4 PM	Philadelphia Eagles	X				X
10/16 SUNDAY	A	4 PM	Kansas City Chiefs	X				X
10/24 MONDAY	A	9 PM	St. Louis Cardinals			X		X
10/30 SUNDAY	H	1 PM	Dallas Cowboys	X				X
11/7 MONDAY	A	9 PM	Detroit Lions			X		X
11/13 SUNDAY	H	4 PM	Washington Redskins	X				X
11/20 SUNDAY	A	1 PM	Philadelphia Eagles	X				X
11/27 SUNDAY	A	4 PM	Los Angeles Raiders	X				X
12/4 SUNDAY	H	1 PM	St. Louis Cardinals	X				X
12/11 SUNDAY	H	1 PM	Seattle Seahawks		X			X
12/17 SATURDAY	A	12:30 PM	Washington Redskins	X				X

171

Irv "kicks off" the publication of his new book.

About The Author

This is Irv Brechner's first book on the light side, his sixth overall. He is the author of the bestselling College Survival Kit, The Career Finder, Getting Into Computers, The Computers Are Coming, The Easy-to-Understand Computer Dictionary and What You Can Do With A Computer.

His advertising/marketing/promotion agency specializes in the personal computer field. He has published this book himself, with the dual purpose of bringing together the stories from the world's largest fraternity and secondly, hoping that a pair of season tickets would someday just show up in the mail!

Future Draft Choice

Every coach dreams about a runner that can do the hundred in lightning speed, cut on the dime and run out of bounds to stop the clock.

Giants management will vouch that people write in with "discoveries" from all over the world—from some hidden mountain town in Colorado to the pyramids of Egypt.

Well, in keeping with the Giants fan tradition of always being on the lookout for top talent, the author has come up with a top draft choice, one which he will sign over to the Giants from free agent status for nothing more than a pair of season tickets . . . make that a box, please!

My prospect can outrun any football player, even the fleet Beasley Reece. He can cut like you wouldn't believe and doesn't require a salary. You see, this prospect is independently wealthy and wants to play ball for the fame. I can see only one potential draw back in Fast Louie, as I call him: his end zone celebration after scoring a touchdown might offend some . . . .

Fast Louie working out at a secret North Jersey high school field. Unknown to pro scouts, Louie might sign out of college and miss his senior year . . .